EVERYDAY GUIDES
MADE EASY

STEP-BY-STEP
SEO
BASICS

RICHARD N. WILLIAMS

FOREWORD BY MARK MAYNE

FLAME TREE
PUBLISHING

CONTENTS

Learn how search engines work, and what search engine optimization is,
why it is important and how it can benefit you.

How do you make a website search engine friendly?
What are keywords and metadata, and how do you use them?

How do you make your website a trusted resource? How important are links,
and how do you get people to link to your website?

Learn how to command authority by growing a community,
encouraging social media shares and releasing news content.

Here we explain how to optimize pages on Amazon, eBay or social media,
as well as tips and techniques to develop your SEO further.

FOREWORD

For generations of people the internet is the primary source of information, and since the late 90s search engines have been one of the most important and widely used ways to navigate the web. Although search engines are no longer the only game in town – thanks to peer-to-peer recommendation and social network growth – they're still highly effective information sources used by millions of people every hour of every day. For example, during Jan 2016 in the US alone 17.5bn searches were made, with Google mopping up 64% of these, followed by Microsoft with 21 per cent.

The art – and science – of creating websites and website content that appears at the top of search engine results listings is called Search Engine Optimisation (SEO), and mastering the concepts behind this ever-evolving skill will give millions of people maximum visibility to your blog or business, often without major expense.

This detailed guide looks at the essential basics of general SEO, as well as providing valuable context of the role SEO should play in a wider brand marketing strategy to give you the best shot at success, no matter what your chosen niche. Whether a gardener or florist, tech blogger, food critic or shoe shop, this book will guide you through the key concepts and practicalities of SEO step-by-step, using clear, concise language and a minimum of jargon.

As well as being intended as a comprehensive primer, you'll also find this guide a helpful reference volume to dip into for one-off queries in the future. So pull up a monitor and mouse, dust off your smartphone, sharpen your mental pencil-box and let's go...SEO!

Mark Mayne Mayne Media

INTRODUCTION

If you have a website or blog, and you want to attract an audience, you need to appear high up in search engine results, and that means your website needs to be optimized. But what is search engine optimization, and how can you go about applying it to your website or blog?

Above: Search engines such as Google use complex algorithms to create search engine results. We'll explain what an algorithm is.

SEARCH ENGINE OPTIMIZATION (SEO)

This book is designed to explain the basics of search engine optimization. What it is, why it is important and how to do it. In short, understanding SEO can help ensure your website, blog or even social media page is attracting its target audience and, just as importantly, ensure your audience keeps coming back to the site.

Keeping it Simple

This book is not designed for the computer expert or internet wizard. Within its pages, you will find simple step-by-step guides to SEO techniques, as well as lots

Hot Tip

Throughout this book, we have inserted a number of Hot Tips. These are designed to help you find some simple yet effective advice about different aspects of search engine optimization.

of useful information about how search engines work.

SEO Reference

You can read this book from cover to cover, or you can use it as a reference guide and turn to it whenever you need help with a different aspect of search engine optimization. This book is designed to help you with SEO for all search engines, whether it is Google, Bing or Yahoo, and even search engines on social media platforms and retail sites, such as Amazon.

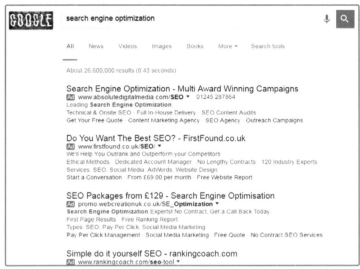

Above: Search engine results often include both sponsored and organic results. In this book, we'll explain the difference.

Jargon Buster

Where possible, we will try to ensure this book is as simple and clear to read as possible, but where complex terms are used, we've included these handy jargon busters.

Above: The techniques in this book are designed to help you optimize your website for all the most commonly used search engines.

WHAT IS SEO?

WHAT IS A SEARCH ENGINE?

If you have ever been on the internet, chances are you have used a search engine. Search engines help us find the information we want, but how do they work, and what are the most popular search engines out there?

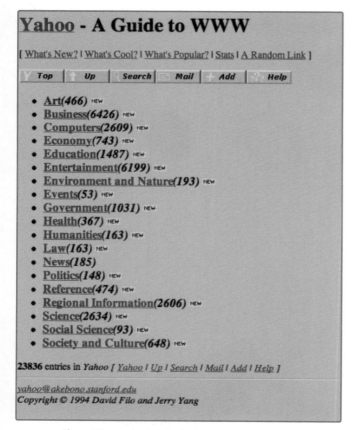

Above: Yahoo used to be a simple directory of web links.

INTERNET SEARCHING

When the World Wide Web first arose, it was very basic. Websites were all connected with hypertext links – text that, when clicked, would take you to another web page or website. A few of the early pioneers created directories of the most popular websites, but finding specific information often meant a lot of trial and error, and clicking back and forth.

First Search Engines

The first search engines emerged in the 1990s. Among them was Yahoo, founded in 1994. Originally, it started as a directory of web pages, but soon evolved to be more sophisticated, enabling users to find specific information by simply typing it into a search box.

FUNCTIONS OF A SEARCH ENGINE

For a search engine to be able to satisfy a search query, it has to be able to do three things:

- **Content Discovery**: A search engine has to find new web pages soon after they appear.

- **Content Indexing**: A search engine has to be able to maintain an index of all the information it has found on the World Wide Web.

- **Search**: Using the index of information, a search engine must be able to offer the most relevant web page to satisfy a user's search.

Above: The search box makes finding information simple and easy.

HOW THEY WORK

Search engines crawl websites. To navigate from web page to web page, a search engine uses links. When it finds a new web page, the search engine adds all the information on it to an index (sometimes called a catalogue). When you conduct a search engine search, you are not actually searching the web but searching an index.

Jargon Buster

Crawling is the term given to the act of a search engine computer program, often called a 'spider' or 'bot', scouring websites, indexing all the information on there.

Despite cautioning site developers from Google to avoid "'free-for-all' links, link popularity schemes, or submitting a site to exercises that don't affect the ranking a site in the results of the major search engines.[5] most[which?] major engines have potentially penalize sites employing such practices.[6]

Acquired link   [edit]

These are the links acquired by the website owner through payment or distribution. They are also known as organically ob linking, article distribution, directory links and comments on forums, blogs and other interactive forms of social media.[7]

Reciprocal link   [edit]

A reciprocal link is a mutual link between two objects, commonly between two websites, to ensure mutual traffic. For exam to Alice's website and Alice's website links to Bob's website, the websites are reciprocally linked. Website owners often sub order to achieve higher rankings in the search engines. Reciprocal linking between websites is no longer an important par with their Jagger 2 update, Google stopped giving credit to reciprocal links as it does not indicate genuine link popularity.[8]

Forum signature linking   [edit]

Forum signature linking is a technique used to build backlinks to a website. This is the process of using forum communitie signature. This can be a fast method to build up inbound links to a website's Search Engine Optimization value.

Blog comments   [edit]

Above: Links often appear in a different colour from normal text.

ALGORITHMS

When a user enters a search query, a search engine lists the results based on how relevant they are to that search. In order to determine relevance, search engines use sophisticated mathematical equations that use hundreds of different factors. These equations are contained in what is known as an algorithm, and they form the backbone of search engines.

Hot Tip

Make sure all your web pages are interconnected with links. Web pages that are not linked to any other web page are called 'orphans' and are not found by search engines.

Ranking

Once a search engine's algorithm has found the most relevant search results, it lists them in what it thinks is the most helpful order. Where a web page appears in a search result is called its 'ranking'. Generally, the higher up the result, the more likely a user is to click on the link to the web page.

About 3,720,000 results (0.92 seconds)

Traditionally a sailing ship (or simply ship) is a sailing vessel that carries three or more masts with square sails on each. Large sailing vessels that are not ship-rigged may be more precisely referred to by their sail rig, such as schooner, **barque** (also spelled "bark"), brig, **barkentine**, brigantine or sloop.

Sailing ship - Wikipedia
https://en.wikipedia.org/wiki/**Sailing_ship**

About this result • Feedback

Sailing ship - Wikipedia
https://en.wikipedia.org/wiki/**Sailing_ship** ▾
Traditionally a sailing ship (or simply ship) is a sailing vessel that carries three or more masts with square sails on each. Large sailing vessels that are not ship-rigged may be more precisely referred to by their sail rig, such as schooner, barque (also spelled "bark"), brig, barkentine, brigantine or sloop.
Characteristics   Types of sailing ships   Automated sailing   Gallery

Images for sailing ships   Report images

More images for sailing ships

Above: Search engines are now very sophisticated and list not just websites but also facts, pictures and other information a user may find interesting.

Determining Rank

Search engines use all sorts of factors to determine the rank of a web page:

- **Popularity:** The most popular websites tend to appear higher up in search results because they have a proven track record of satisfying user searches.

- **Links:** Websites that have lots of inbound links (links from other websites) tend to rank highly.

Hot Tip

The higher up the search engine rankings, the better. If you have a web page on page two of Google, getting it on page one will bring a dramatic improvement in traffic.

Above: Where a website appears on a search engine results page is known as its ranking.

○ **Content:** Good-quality content that is informative and detailed ranks better than thin content that offers little value to searchers.

○ **Relevance:** How relevant a web page is to a user's search also affects its rank.

POPULAR SEARCH ENGINES

Three big names dominate the world of search engines, and together they receive 97 per cent of all internet searches.

- **Google**: By far the world's most popular search engine, Google is used by around two thirds of all internet users.

- **Bing**: Microsoft's Bing is the world's second most popular search engine, used by around a fifth of internet users.

- **Yahoo**: Attracting 10 per cent of users, Yahoo is the third most popular search engine, but also has the honour of being the oldest.

- **Others**: Other search engines include AOL, Ask.com, Excite and Baidu.

Above: Ask.com used to be called Ask Jeeves.

Above: Baidu is the most popular search engine in China.

WHAT IS SEO?

SEO, or search engine optimization, is a way of ensuring your website or blog appears as high up in the rankings as possible. By ranking higher, you receive more traffic and reach a wider audience.

RANKING IS EVERYTHING

Where a web page appears in a search engine's ranking has a dramatic effect on the number of people who visit that web page. The top result on a search engine results page usually gets more traffic than the second result, which gets more traffic than the third result, and so on.

Hot Tip

Fewer than 10 per cent of people click to page two of search engine results, making getting your website on page one crucial for attracting an audience.

Get Your Website Found Online. - Request Your Free SEO Review.
Ad www.altitude-internet-**seo**.co.uk/fast/**seo** ▾
Request Your Free **SEO** Review Now. We'll Call You Back For A Chat. UK Based Team.
First Class Service. - Get On Googles 1st Page.

Searches related to seo websites

seo **website design**	**search engine optimization techniques**
search engine optimization google	**search engine optimization for dummies**
how to do search engine optimization	how to do seo **yourself**
search engine optimization tools	**search engine optimization tips**

Goooooooooogle ›
1 2 3 4 5 6 7 8 9 10   Next

Left: A search query may generate hundreds of pages of results, but few people ever click past the first one or two pages.

Search Results

Search engines such as Google, Yahoo and Bing divide search results into two types:

○ **Paid Search**: These are web pages that the website owner has paid to appear in the search results for a particular search term. They are usually denoted by a symbol.

○ **Organic Results**: These are web pages that the search engine deems most relevant to a search term.

About 546,000,000 results (0.66 seconds)

SEO Services That Perform - The Award Winning SEO Company
Ad www.absolutedigitalmedia.com/**SEO**-Agency/UK ▼ 01245 287864
SEO Campaigns With Proven Results. 97% Client Retention Rate. Get a Quote Today.
SEO Content Audits · Technical & Onsite SEO · Full In-House Delivery · Expert SEO Campaigns
Services · SEO Outreach Campaigns, Technical SEO, Link Building, Complete Website SEO
    SEO Agency   Content Marketing Agency
    Outreach Campaigns   Get Your Free Quote

Take an instant SEO review - We'll help maximise your reach
Ad www.omnidigitalmarketing.co.uk/free-**seo**-audit ▼ 0114 349 0785
We deliver tailored **SEO** solutions that will help you challenge your competitors.
Fantastic ROI · Based in Yorkshire · Incredible Track Record · Free SEO Review
Services: Web Design, SEO, Pay Per Click, Content Writing, Social Media Management

Fast Low Cost SEO That Works. - Thousands Of Clients Across UK
Ad www.boost-local.co.uk/lowcost/**seo** ▼ 0800 234 3001
Low Cost **SEO**. No Contracts. Cancel Anytime. Great Service & Great Value **SEO**
Low Cost Effective SEO · Contact Us Right Now · About Boost Local SEO · Sign Up Right Now

Get Your Website Found Online. - Request Your Free SEO Review.
Ad www.altitude-internet-**seo**.co.uk/fast/**seo** ▼
Professional **SEO** Services To Get Your Website On Page 1 Of The Search Engines.

SEO: The Beginner's Guide to Search Engine Optimization - Moz
https://moz.com/beginners-guide-to-**seo** ▼
18 Dec 2015 - The Beginner's Guide to **SEO** has been read over 3 million times and provides
comprehensive information you need to get on the road to professional quality Search Engine
Optimization, or **SEO**. ... **SEO** is a marketing discipline focused on growing visibility in organic (non-

Above: On Google, adverts are distinguishable from organic search results by the green 'Ad' symbol.

Organic Results

While you can pay to have your web page appear high up in search results, paid search results – as opposed to organic search results – receive only 10 per cent of traffic, making organic traffic far more powerful in generating an audience.

Jargon Buster

Search engine results pages are often referred to as SERPS.

SEARCH ENGINE OPTIMIZATION

When we talk about search engine optimization (SEO), we are only talking about optimizing web pages to help them appear higher up in organic search results. To appear high up in paid-for listings requires increasing the payments made to the search engine companies.

Tips, Tricks and Tactics

All sorts of SEO techniques, tactics and strategies can be used to optimize a web page, but they often fall into three areas:

- **White Hat**: These are techniques aimed at putting the human audience first, and abiding by the guidelines published by search engine companies.

- **Black Hat**: These are aggressive SEO techniques designed to fool search engines, and are quite often against search engine rules and guidelines.

- **Grey (Gray) Hat**: Somewhere in the middle, usually employing techniques that, while not against search engine guidelines, are still attempting to play the system.

| All | Shopping | Images | News | Videos | More ▾ | Search tools |

About 480,000,000 results (0.51 seconds)

Looking For SEO Backlinks? - Fast Delivery. Quality Content
Ad content.ocere.com/BloggerOutreach/Guest-Blogging ▾ 01242 525557
Choose Metrics: Da, Pr, Social Etc. Hundreds of Sites, Contact Now!
High Quality Content · 100% White Label · Choose Your Metrics · No Contract
Services: High Quality Links, Blogger Outreach, White Label SEO, Infographic Placement, Tier 2 Link ...

    Get Underway Today   Blogger Outreach Service
    Backlinking Service   Link Outreaching Service

Buy Backlinks Here - $15 to $167 backlink packages
Ad www.fullturnmarketing.com/ ▾
Buy Your Backlinks From Us. Satisfaction Guaranteed. High Quality Backlinks.
No Taxes · Various Sizes · Free Shipping · Multiple Colors
100,000 Backlinks · Monthly SEO Backlinks · High Quality Backlinks · Buy Cheap Backlinks

Backlinks.com - Buy & Sell Quality Backlinks
www.backlinks.com/ ▾
Join the hundreds of thousands of users who are **buying** and selling **links** through BackLinks.
Sell Text Links · Affiliate Program · Improve Your SERP's with One ... · Register Here

Should You Buy Backlinks? | SEOmark ©
www.seomark.co.uk/**buy-backlinks**/ ▾
The problem? Google clearly states that **buying** backlinks to improve your rankings breaches their guidelines. They consider **links** as votes and that paying for a ...

Hot Tip

To prevent people from playing the system, search engines often make dramatic changes to their algorithms, which can send web pages that have used black-hat techniques plummeting down the rankings.

Left: Lots of websites offer to sell links, but doing this sort of black-hat SEO can get you penalized in the rankings or even omitted from search results altogether.

HOMECOMING   PROM   FORMAL   UNDER $100   PLUS   SHOE

PLUS SIZE PROM DRESSES AND **PLUS SIZE** EVENING

Prom Girl is your source for **plus size** homecoming dresses, **plus size** prom dresses an gowns. Whether you are looking for a cheap **plus size** prom dress or **plus size** formal w dresses to fit **plus size** girls. You will find many beautiful **plus size** formal evening gown you are looking for a cheap **plus size** prom dress, you will find many of our beautiful dre are quite reasonable.

Above: Overusing keywords in an attempt to please a search engine makes content read poorly and may not help with SEO.

Convincing the Algorithms

Many people confuse SEO with trying to trick a search engine into believing a web page is worthy of ranking higher than it actually is. In fact, SEO is about ensuring your web page satisfies potential search requests. While it is possible to fool a search engine into ranking a web page highly, search engines often penalize those who have used aggressive SEO (black hat) techniques. A good rule of thumb is to make sure you are thinking of human users, not search engine bots, when applying SEO.

THE IMPORTANCE OF SEO

Search engines have to find the most relevant web pages to suit search requests among the billions of pages in existence. That is no easy task. SEO ensures your web page is easily read by search engines and satisfies a user's search, giving it the best chance of appearing high up in the rankings.

WHY SEO?

Because most people find web content through search engines, anything you can do to improve your chances of ranking higher drives more traffic to your site and increases visibility. The higher you rank, the more visitors your website or blog receives. For instance, SEO can help a web page appearing on page two for a specific search query, and receiving only a handful of visitors each day, appear on page one, increasing the number of visitors into the hundreds or even thousands.

Google | plumber

All   Maps   Images   N

About 106,000,000 results (0.81 s

The Local Plumbers. - F
Ad www.thelocalplumbers.co.

Above: A search may bring up millions of results, so unless you rank near the top, few people will find your website.

Machine Eyes

While a website may appear to be well written and full of great content, search engines are not like humans, and sometimes struggle to understand a web page and who it is aimed at. SEO can help search engines work out what the web page is about and how useful it is for a specific search term, and generate the traffic it deserves.

Ahead of the Competition

If you have a business website or blog, SEO can make a big difference. If two websites are selling the same product or service, one that is search engine optimized will attract more customers and make more sales than a non-optimized website.

Other Benefits of SEO

SEO provides lots of advantages. Not only can it lead to more traffic to your website, but it can also have other effects:

Above: Search engines such as Google often offer ways to help businesses appear in local searches, such as placement on maps (more on this in Advanced SEO, page 82).

- **Snowball Search Rankings:** When you increase web traffic through SEO, more people visit your site. This in turn makes your website more appealing to search engines, further boosting your rankings.

Above: Adverts on search engines cost money every time somebody clicks on the website link. Clicks on organic links cost nothing.

- ◎ **Boost Branding**: The more people who visit your website, the more familiar it will become. If it is a business website or blog, this will boost your brand.

- ◎ **Free**: While it is possible to attract visitors to your website using advertising, this costs money. Organic SEO does not have any fixed costs attached.

SEO GOALS

For many people, the ultimate goal is to get on page one of a search engine such as Google. For some very competitive search terms, this may not always be possible. However, SEO can still bring rewards in increased traffic, and you can even adopt an SEO strategy to target relevant but less common search terms, gaining you large numbers of extra visitors.

SEO GOOD PRACTICE

SEO practices are not only beneficial for search engines, but following basic SEO techniques can help improve the user experience and usability of a website. An optimized website often reads better to human visitors, is laid out in a better way, and encourages more people to stay or revisit it in the future.

Hot Tip

Search engines now categorize content so users can carry out separate searches for products, news, images, videos and even books.

Abiding by the Rules

By following basic white-hat SEO principles, you can ensure your website does not accidentally run foul of search engine penalties. Search engines often demote websites for bad practice, weak content and poor user experiences.

Designed to enhance driveway , entryways, gardens, or your entire home in general. All of our Aluminum or Wrought Iron Gates, or Fences are designed and manufactured to withstand a range of outdoor conditions. Our commitment to our customers and dedication to produce quality gates has earned us thousands of satisfied customers.

Although we offer a wide selection or Ornamental Designs or Decorative Designs, we can design and manufacture any style in aluminum or wrought iron metals. L. A. Ornamental & Rack Corp also offers Fences, Garden or Walk Thru Gates to match your driveway gates. With over thirty five years of experience in manufacturing and designing elegant, custom, or exotic Aluminum Driveway Gates and Fences, our past and future customers can have peace of mind that they are receiving quality workmanship. We are a Fence Company that gives our customers 110% of dedication to manufacture quality driveway gates and fences. For a quote please send an e-mail to LAOrnamental@aol.com

If your looking For Privacy with your Driveway Gates ,Garden Gates, or Walk Thru Gates, we offer a Solid Backing with your choice of Aluminium, Steel, Plexiglas or Plastic. All solid backing are offered in many different colors to choose from. Privacy Gates

We offer a large selection of Gate Openers and Gate Operators for Residential Driveway Gates, Light or Heavy Commercial Gates, or industrial locations. If your not sure the style or size of the Gate opener / gate operator you need, please e-mail or contact us so we can gladly help guide you to the correct choice. We offer all type of Gate Openers / Gate Operator, Sliding Gate Openers / Gate

Welding Expertise

nd Gate Operators
laster Gate Openers
ate Operators
te Openers
Gate Operators

Above: An understanding of the principles of SEO can help websites with poor design such as this improve the look and user experience.

OUTSOURCING SEO

SEO can seem like a daunting and complicated subject. Indeed, many people wanting to improve their search rankings often outsource their website SEO to third parties. However, SEO is really not that difficult, and doing it yourself has many advantages.

- **Cost**: Professional SEO companies charge high prices for their services. If you only have a small website or blog, this may prove far too costly.

- **Control**: Some third-party SEO companies use aggressive (black hat) SEO techniques to get speedy results. This can often lead to a website eventually being penalized in search engine rankings.

- **Knowledge**: Learning how to do SEO gives you a better understanding of internet practices and how websites should be constructed.

About 4,390,000 results (0.47 seconds)

SEO Services That Perform - The Award Winning SEO Company
Ad www.absolutedigitalmedia.com/**SEO**-Services ▾
SEO Marketing Campaigns With Proven Results. Are You Missing Out? We Can Help
Expert SEO Campaigns · Full In-House Delivery · Technical & Onsite SEO · SEO Content Audits
    Outreach Campaigns   Content Marketing Agency
    The Award Winning Agency   SEO Agency

Affordable SEO Services - Increase Your Organic Traffic
Ad www.bubblegumsearch.com/**services**/**seo** ▾   020 8191 7373
Free SEO Audit. No Fixed Contract. Boutique SEO Agency.
Agency Expertise · Boutique Service · Bespoke Strategies
Contact · Our Services · SEO · Content Marketing

Award Winning SEO Services - Vertical Leap - vertical-leap.uk
Ad www.vertical-leap.uk/**SEO**/**Service** ▾
Our In-House SEO Software Puts Us Way Ahead Of The Game, Talk To Us Today.
Web & Digital Design · Get In touch · SEO · PPC · Social Media Services · Content Creation

Chillibyte SEO Agency - Boutique Search Agency - Chillibyte.co.uk
Ad www.chillibyte.co.uk/**SEO**-Agency ▾
Monthly SEO Fees from £600
Effective SEO Solutions · No Minimum Contract · Free SEO Audit · 95% Customer Retention

Guaranteed SEO | Juicy Results
www.juicyresults.com/**guaranteed-seo**/ ▾

Above: Lots of companies offer SEO services, but doing it yourself not only saves money but also ensures you do not fall foul of search engine rules.

THE BUILDING BLOCKS OF SEO

Now you know what SEO is and how important it is for attracting an audience to your website or blog, let's look at the different elements that make up good search engine optimization.

ELEMENTS OF SEO

Although SEO can appear complex, and the algorithms that drive search engines work differently to one another and change frequently, the fundamental principles of SEO remain the same, and can be summed up in three words:

- **Relevance**: Is your website or blog relevant to what a user has searched for?

- **Trust**: Can a search engine trust that your website will provide relevant, useful content?

- **Authority**: Does your website or blog command authority? Is it popular?

Above: Wikipedia always appears high up in search results because it offers good-quality, trusted and authoritative content.

Relevance

We will look at what makes a web page relevant in 'A Search-Engine Friendly Site' (pages 32-41) but, in essence, you cannot expect to appear high in SERPS if your content does not satisfy a user's search request. After all, how frustrating would it be to type 'local plumber' into a search box and get a website for a florist?

Jargon Buster

A webmaster is somebody who maintains a website. They may be the person who built the website or simply the administrator.

Trust

In the early days of search engines, it was easy for unscrupulous webmasters to play the system, buying links that would make a website appear more popular than it actually was. These days, search engines are far more sophisticated, and links have to come from natural sources, from people who have found your content useful (we cover this in more detail in the section 'Building A Trusted Site', page 62).

Quick Buy Backlink Services

We've developed a variety of backlink services for any type of website. Browse each section below, we're sure there is something there you'll like.

Above: Some websites sell backlinks, but these are unlikely to fool a search engine.

Authority

Not only do search engines want your content to be trustworthy and relevant, but it needs to command authority too. How a search engine determines authority is based on several factors – primarily how popular it is and the types of websites that link to your site.

For instance, a backlink from a university or a national news organization commands more authority than a backlink from a friend's Facebook page (see the section on 'Commanding Authority', page 82).

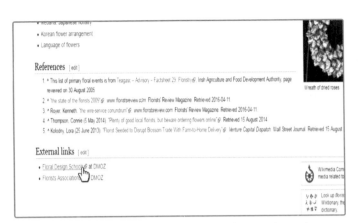

Above: Backlinks from authoritative sources such as Wikipedia are worth more than backlinks from a regular blog or website.

ON-PAGE AND OFF-PAGE SEO

SEO often falls into two categories, and both are as equally important as the other if you want to appear high in search engine rankings.

○ **On-page SEO**: This refers to SEO techniques that you apply to your website, such as keywords, use of headers, URL structure and optimized page layout.

○ **Off-page SEO**: This refers to things outside of your website that can improve your rankings, such as link building and social media shares.

Jargon Buster

A backlink is a link that comes from an external website, taking a user to your site. Search engines use backlinks as a measure of popularity.

RULES OF THE GAME

In essence, good SEO is all about following the rules and guidelines published by search engines. While these differ, they share several basic tenets:

Above: Make sure a user can find all the pages on your website simply and easily.

- **Information**: Give visitors the information they're looking for.

- **High Quality**: Make sure content is high quality and useful.

- **Clear**: Make it easy to find the information a user is looking for. Ensure you use keywords (more on this in 'Keywords', page 42).

Above: Google uses a highly sophisticated algorithm to discover more about your website.

- **Links**: Make sure other sites link to yours.

- **Accessible**: Your site should have a logical structure so a user can reach every page quickly and easily.

- **Clean**: Your website needs to be clear of clutter, easy to navigate and quick to load.

Hot Tip

Google uses an algorithm called PageRank to determine how important, authoritative and reliable a website is for a user. PageRank gives each website a score from one to 10 (10 being the most valuable).

Above: You can use online tools to check your website's PageRank.

A SEARCH-ENGINE FRIENDLY SITE

SEARCH-ENGINE FRIENDLY CONTENT

People use search engines to find all sorts of content, from articles and information to pictures and videos, but what makes content search-engine friendly? And do you have to make a compromise between content for search engines and content for a human audience?

CONTENT IS KING

The World Wide Web is all about content. Whenever people use a search engine, they are looking for content, but content takes many forms, from articles and news stories to how-to blogs, videos and podcasts. Whatever type of content you are providing, you need to ensure people can find it – and that means making it search-engine friendly.

Above: Search engine results are not just full of written articles, but adverts, videos and images often appear in the rankings too.

SEO Content

Nearly all types of content can be optimized for search engines. Here is how:

- **Articles:** Whether you are producing news stories, interviews, features or even recipes, the web is full of useful articles on every subject imaginable, so you need to ensure yours can be easily found.

- **Product Pages**: E-commerce sites contain descriptions of products and services, but customers will find those pages that have been optimized first.

- **Blog Posts**: Whether it is a business blog or a place to share an opinion or discuss an interest or hobby, there is no point in having a blog if people can't find it.

- **Multimedia**: Videos, images and podcasts can all be optimized too, so they appear high in the rankings.

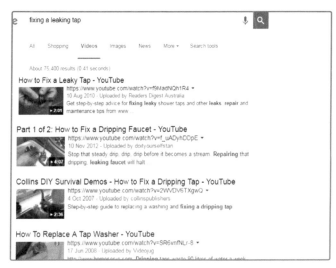

Above: Users can now conduct separate image and video searches.

Be Obvious

Both users and search engines need to know what your website or blog is about and the type of content that appears on it. If you provide news, ensure you say so on your website; if your blog is about a particular topic, make sure that is clear. You should also explain what your content includes – videos, articles, images, reviews and so on – because this ensures that not only do search engines know what is on your web page but that visitors know they have come to the right place, too.

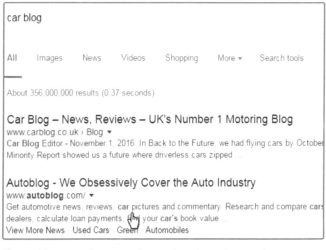

Above: Make sure search engines and your audience know what type of content is contained on your blog or website.

KNOW YOUR AUDIENCE

Before you embark on optimizing your website or blog, you need to make sure you know at whom you are aiming your content. You need to ensure you know the types of people you are trying to attract. Think about who they might be, so you can be sure you are putting out the right type of content for them.

- **Demographics:** Is your audience a specific age group? Gender? Are they professionals, experts or novices?

- **Needs:** What type of content is your audience looking for – products, advice, useful information or multimedia?

- **Competition:** What other websites does your audience visit? If they cannot find the content they are looking for with you, where else will they get it?

Ability Plumbing and Heating Engineers Kent: Ability UK
www.ability.uk.com/
We are a local family business who pride ourselves on providing a fast, efficient, quality **plumbing** and central heating service in the Kent, Sussex (East and ...

Pimlico Plumbers | Plumbers London Emergency Plumbers London ...
www.pimlico**plumbers**.com/ ▾
Plumbing and gas heating engineers. Profile and services.

Plumber - National Careers Service - Gov.uk
https://nationalcareersservice.direct.gov.uk/job-profiles/**plumber** ▾
11 Oct 2016 - **Plumbers** fit and service heating systems. They also repair faults in hot and cold water supplies and drainage networks.

Plumber - Wikipedia
https://en.wikipedia.org/wiki/**Plumber** ▾
A **plumber** is a tradesperson who specializes in installing and maintaining systems used for potable (drinking) water, sewage and drainage in **plumbing** systems.

Plumbers in UK | MyBuilder
https://www.mybuilder.com › Find Tradesmen ▾
Read reviews and hire expert **Plumbers** in UK for leaks, piping, toilet installations, soil pipes and more.

Above: Check out the competition. See what content they are producing and how you can match or even better it.

Hot Tip

The demographics of your audience can make a big difference to the type of content they may expect to see. Younger audiences may like short articles, videos and podcasts, while older visitors may like more in-depth articles.

Tone of Voice

It is important to ensure you are writing in the correct tone of voice for your audience. Even if your website audience is professional or knowledgeable, avoid sounding too formal or technical. You want to make your content as engaging and informative as possible to as many people as possible. Explain jargon and technical phrases if you want to attract and keep new visitors.

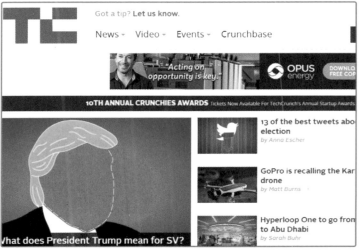

Above: Even technical websites, such as TechCrunch, ensure their content is easy to read and accessible to expert and novice alike.

SEO CONTENT STRATEGY

Once you have identified your audience, you need to identify your goals. It is not enough just to say you want to appear on page one of Google, or be in the top three organic search results. You need to decide why you want to be in that position in order to plan your SEO strategy.

- **Sales**: If you are trying to drive product sales, you need attractive, informative product pages, with clear descriptions.

- **Blogs**: To achieve a larger blog audience, you need to ensure your content is informative and useful, with catchy headlines and an easy-to-read structure.

- **Advertising**: If you want to bring an audience to your website so you can earn money from advertisers, focus on headlines that will attract page views, but avoid clickbait.

Thursday, September 29, 2016

You'll Never Guess What Happens Next When Big Brother Casts Pretty Girls!

I love this season!!

Above: Avoid sensationalist clickbait headlines. They may attract page views, but visitors will soon disappear again.

Jargon Buster

Clickbait is content that is designed just to encourage visitors to click it, often with provocative headlines, but the content can often fail to live up to its promises, and visitors may never return.

Editorial Calendar

Both search engines and human readers like new content. If you are not updating your content regularly, your visitors will stop coming back, and your rankings will fall in the SERPS as you lose popularity. An editorial calendar helps you schedule new content and gives you deadlines to come up with new content ideas.

Analyse Success

You need to ensure you know what content is working and what isn't, both for search engines and your audience. Study what works, repeat similar content, and update older content to make it more attractive to both search engines and your audience (more on measuring success and analytics in 'Advanced SEO', page 122).

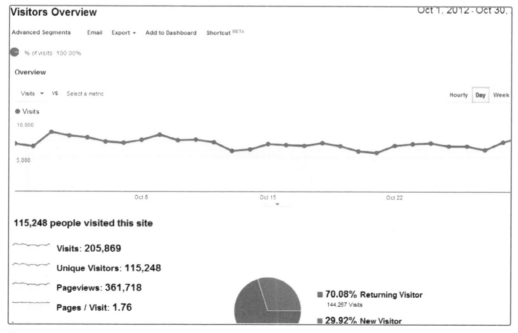

Above: Keeping track of your page visits helps you determine whether your SEO strategy is working.

SEARCH-ENGINE FRIENDLY CONTENT

One of the most common mistakes people make when optimizing websites for search engines is focusing too much on what they think search engines want to see, and forgetting their audience. The key thing to remember is to write for your audience first and foremost.

Matching Searches

To appear relevant to search engines, your content has to appeal to what people are searching for.

- **Keywords**: What are the words and phrases people type into search engines to find content like yours? (More on keywords in the next section, page 42.)

Hyundai IONIQ - The Newest in Electric Cars - hyundai-ioniq.com
Ad www.hyundai-ioniq.com/Hyundai/IONIQ ▾
Innovative, Efficient, Powertrain Technology. Test Drive Hyundai IONIQ Today.
Smart Technology · Intelligent Safety System · Regenerative Breaking · 5 Year Warranty
Find the Perfect Car · Locate Nearest Dealer · Hyundai Brochures · Book a Test Drive

Read on for our guide to the ten best electric cars for sale in the UK today.

- Renault ZOE hatchback. ...
- Hyundai Ioniq hatchback. ...
- Tesla Model S hatchback. ...
- Tesla Model X SUV. ...
- BMW i3 hatchback. ...
- Nissan Leaf hatchback. ...
- Volkswagen e-Golf hatchback. ...
- Kia Soul hatchback.

More items...

Best electric cars of 2016 revealed | Carbuyer
www.carbuyer.co.uk/reviews/recommended/**best-electric-cars**

About this result · Feedback

Above: Some search engines now include a 'featured snippet', where an excerpt of what it considers the most relevant content appears in the search results.

- **Queries**: Does your content answer questions or queries that people type into search engines?

- **Information**: Are you providing information that people commonly use search engines to find?

SEARCH-ENGINE VISIBILITY

Simply providing relevant content is not enough to ensure you are visible to search engines. Search engines do not read a website in the same way a person does, so it has to be structured in a way that ensures they can index it effectively.

Clarity

Clarity is crucial if you want search engines to match your web page with a relevant search request.

- **Subject**: Make sure it is clear what your web page is about. Use headers (titles) and sub-headings.

Above: Avoid cluttered websites or blogs. Keep the structure clean.

- **Focused:** Keep each page focused on a single subject or aspect of your subject.

- **Make Content Key:** Do not litter your pages with adverts or embedded applications. Make sure the content is dominant.

Above: Clean, well-structured websites make it easy for search engines to crawl them.

Site Structure

Ensure your website is well structured, so search engine spiders can crawl it easily. Use indexes, sitemaps, titles, tags and metadata (more on this in 'Build SEO-Friendly Sites', page 53).

Stay Fresh

Information quickly becomes outdated on the web, so ensure you keep publishing new content. Major search engines such as Google use freshness to rank pages. Think of search engine rankings like top 10 lists at a bookshop or record store. Even the most popular titles eventually fall down the rankings as new releases come out.

Hot Tip

Avoid duplicate content. Search engines do not like content that is repeated elsewhere. If need be, link to an article. Never cut and paste content from somewhere else.

KEYWORDS

If you want your web pages to match search results, you need to understand keywords: what they are, how to use them, how to find the right ones to use, and how not to use them.

KEYWORDS EXPLAINED

As discussed in previous sections, search engines use all sorts of criteria to match a search request with relevant content. One of these criteria, and traditionally one of the most important, is keywords.

Put simply, keywords are words or phrases entered into a search box that match the words or phrases in your content.

Example: A user types 'plumber in London' into Google. Google searches the index for all web pages that contain the words 'plumber' and 'London'.

Plumber in London - Find a trade with Checkatrade.
www.checkatrade.com/Search/**Plumber/in/London** ▾
All members providing **Plumber** services in **London** are Recommended, Vet
meet our standards of trading.

London Plumbers | aspect.co.uk
www.aspect.co.uk/**plumbing**/ ▾
London plumbers on call 24 hours a day, seven days a week on 0843 216
knowledgeable, honest". We're here, and we'd love to help.

Plumbers and plumbing service in London - Gumtree
https://www.gumtree.com/**plumbing**-services/**london** ▾
Find a **plumber** or an engineer available in **London** on Gumtree. Services in
plumbing and heating works, boiler installation, gas safe and ...

Above: Search engines match the keywords entered into a search box with those used on a web page.

Search Strings

When somebody enters more than one word into a search engine query box, it is known as a search string. It is worth noting that search engines rank web pages based on how many of these words are in the content, in whatever order. The more of the words entered that are present, the closer the search engine regards it as a match. Search strings placed between 'speech marks' are known as phrase searches, and are matched exactly, so if that exact phrase is not on your web page, the search engine doesn't bring it up.

IMPORTANCE OF KEYWORDS

Keywords used to be the single most important aspect of SEO. When algorithms were less sophisticated, search engines used to rank pages with the highest number of matching keywords on a page. This resulted in many webmasters creating web content with the same words and phrases repeatedly throughout, often ruining the user experience.

Hot Tip

Search engines tend to ignore prepositions, conjunctions and other connecting words unless the search request has been placed in speech marks.

Your search - **"florists and floral arrangements in london"** - did not match any documents.

Suggestions:

- Make sure that all words are spelled correctly.
- Try different keywords.
- Try more general keywords.

Pulbrook & Gould Flowers - World renowned florist in Sloane St
Ad www.pulbrookandgould.co.uk/ ▾
Luxurious bouquets for delivery

1800FLOWERS® Arrangements
Ad www.1800flowers.com/International ▾
4.5 ★★★★✯ rating for 1800flowers.com
Shop Elegant Floral Arrangements. International & Worldwide Delivery
Truly original gifts · Deliver to 190+ countries · Fresh flower guarantee · 24 x 7 toll-free number
Types: Bouquets, Baskets, Gifts, Gourmet Food

Luxury Flowers London
Ad www.wildthingsflowers.co.uk/ ▾
Order online Now. Same-day delivery Mayfair's finest local Florist
Flower Delivery · Corporate Flowers · Funeral Flowers · Wedding Flowers
The Lilac Garden · The Bentley Collection · Crimson And Violet · Vintage Pinks · Services · Ivory

Above: A phrase match in quotes has to match exactly.

Why Budgeting Your Auto Insurance Quote Can Save You Money

Posted by Julio on 15 June 2016, 9:13 pm

Publicaciones reci
› Why Budgeting Your Aut
Quote Can Save You Mone
› What Are The Types Of C
Insurance
› Get Easy Car Insurance Q
› How To Find Budget-frie
Insurance
› Quote Your Vehicle Insur

Budget Your Auto Insurance Quote Online

A long time back, individuals needed to go to insurance agency workplaces and to get a quote that way. These days, with the always upsetting Web, you can now get a auto insurance quote online, which can spare time. This is a much speedier technique also and should be possible at whatever time of the day or even at night. You get corresponded with several organizations from everywhere throughout the nation that **can offer scope** instead of simply your neighborhood.

An auto insurance quote online is perfect for getting you **acclimated** to your value go each month of what you are going to pay for scope. You can see what is secured in your quote and after that settle on a definite choice of what you need to do. More individuals love the comfort that the Web brings to the table. Exchanging insurance agencies can spare you a couple of hundred dollars **a year**, and some will bring down your premium after a specific measure of time.

Filed under Insurance Quotes | Tagged a car insurance, affordable car insurance quotes, auto insurance free quote, auto insurance online quote, auto insurance rate quote, automobile insurance policy, automotive insurance quote, budget car insurance quote, car insurance group, car insurance quick quote, car insurance sites, check car insurance online, comprehensive car insurance quote, free auto insurance quote online, free automobile insurance quotes, free online auto insurance quotes, get a auto insurance quote, get a car quote, get auto insurance quote, get auto insurance quotes online, get free insurance quote, instant car insurance quotes, instant online car insurance quote, insurance car comparison, insurance quote for car, online auto insurance quote

Above: Keyword stuffing is likely to get you penalized in search engine rankings, rather than boost SEO.

Keyword Stuffing

Algorithms are far more sophisticated now, and not only does keyword stuffing have little effect on a page's rank, but quite often search engines penalize pages that are considered to have too many keywords repeated throughout the content.

Semantics

Not only do you not need to stuff your content with the same words over and over again, but search engines are also sophisticated enough now to be able to identify the semantics of words and phrases. In other words, search engines put more emphasis on the meaning of words rather than the words themselves.

Jargon Buster

Keyword stuffing is the practice of cramming the same keywords repeatedly into content in the hope of appearing more relevant to search engines.

Example: If you type 'dripping tap' into Google, you may find your search results are full of plumbers. Some of the pages will have the keywords 'dripping tap' in the content, while others might have variations, such as 'leaking tap'. Other pages may not contain any of the words at

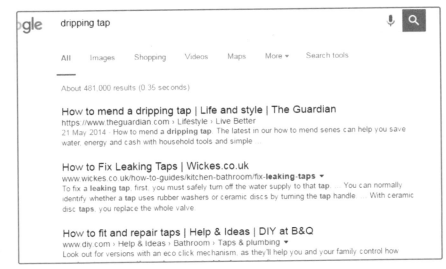

Above: Search engines understand that different words can mean similar things, such as 'leaking' and 'dripping'.

all but, because the search engine connects that phrase with plumbers and plumbing, it brings up the page as being relevant.

LONG-TAIL KEYWORDS

People don't just type words and short phrases into search engines. Sometimes, they type whole sentences or long phrases. These are known as long-tail keywords and, broadly, they can fall into two categories:

- **Descriptive Phrases**: These can include things such as location, colours, types and styles of items – for example, 'contemporary leather three piece suite for sale'.

- **Questions**: Some people use search engines to find the answer to a specific question, such as, 'What is the tallest building in London called?'

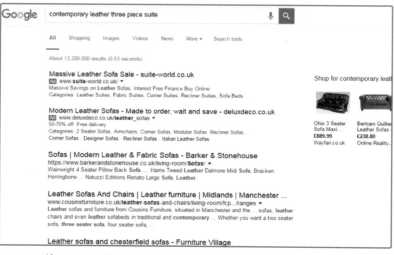

Above: Long-tail keyword searches bring up more precise results.

Above: Answering a long-tail question is a good way of getting content high up in search engine results.

Advantages of Long-Tail Keywords

When it comes to optimizing your web pages, thinking about long-tail keywords does hold an advantage over optimizing for shorter keywords: less competition. Appearing near the top of the search engine rankings for common keywords such as 'plumber', 'florist' or 'furniture shop' is near to impossible, due to the sheer number of websites that contain those words. By expanding your focus to include long-tail keywords, you have more chance of appearing higher in the rankings, as well as attracting visitors whose specific demands you can match more closely.

KEYWORD STRATEGY

Identifying the sorts of words and phrases people use to search for content that matches your website or blog is one of the big challenges of SEO, but there are several methods to identify what keywords to use:

Related Searches

Some search engines – Google, in particular – can help you identify keywords by using their auto-complete and related searches facility.

1. Type the most obvious keywords related to your blog or website content into Google, such as 'plumber', 'florist' or 'politics'.

2. Look at the auto-complete suggestions as you type.

3. After completing a search, scroll down the first page of search engine results until you see 'Searches related to …' and note the keyword phrases.

Hot Tip

If you have an information website or blog, using questions as your article headings or blog entries is a good way of ensuring you appear high in the rankings if people ever type these questions into search boxes.

Google
plumber

plumbers **near me**
plumbers
plumbers **merchants**
plumbers **mate**

Press Enter to search.

Above: Looking at auto-complete suggestions is a good way to identify related keywords.

Kent / Sussex Plumbing Service - Repairs and Installations
Ad www.pjclifford.com/ ▾
Emergency Call Outs - Gas Safe. 24 hour service. Gas, combi & oil boilers

Searches related to plumber

recommended plumbers tunbridge wells   jd plumbing tunbridge wells
emergency plumber tunbridge wells   ability plumbers tunbridge wells
john harris plumber tunbridge wells   pantiles plumbing
plumbing supplies tunbridge wells   plumber tonbridge

Goooooooooogle >
1 2 3 4 5 6 7 8 9 10   Next

Above: Related searches show you what other similar keywords people are using.

Hot Tip

Most search engines do not distinguish between UK and US spellings, and can identify common spelling mistakes and typos.

Keyword Research Tools

You can also use a keyword research tool:

○ **Keyword Tool (http://keywordtool.io):** A free, easy-to-use keyword research tool that enables you to find the most common keywords for Google, Bing, YouTube, Amazon and App Store.

Right: Keyword Tool also has a premium service, enabling you to get more keyword results.

Jargon Buster

AdWords is Google's pay-per-click (PPC) advertising service, which lets you list advertisements in search engine results.

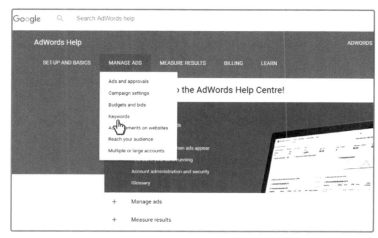

Above: Google's Keyword Planner is designed for use with PPC adverts but works just as well for finding organic keywords.

- **Google Keyword Planner (https://adwords.google.co.uk/KeywordPlanner):** If you have an AdWords account, you can sign in and use Google's Keyword Planner.

- **Moz (https://moz.com):** This paid-for analytics service lets you try out its easy-to-use keyword checker for free. It not only gives keyword suggestions, but also provides all sorts of statistics and analytics.

Right: Moz's SEO tool for finding keywords is available as a free 30-day trial.

USING KEYWORDS

Once you have identified the best keywords related to your website or blog, you need to learn how to use them. In the old days of SEO, when search engines were less sophisticated, it didn't matter how or where you placed keywords, or how many you used, but this is no longer the case.

Hot Tip

Avoid using the same keywords and phrases too often. Think of variations and semantic alternatives. For example, instead of using 'laptop repair', use 'computer fix'.

Natural Placement

When you are writing content, you should use keywords naturally; do not force them into the text. Content should read well to human visitors, not just search engines. If it doesn't fit naturally in the text, it may be an indication that the keyword is unsuitable for that web page. It is important only to use keywords that fit with what your content is about.

Above: Keywords should be placed naturally, not forced into the text.

Density

When using keywords, you must use them sparingly. Cramming too many into your content could result in your web page being penalized in the rankings for keyword stuffing. A good rule of thumb is not to use the same keyword phrase more than two or three times on a page.

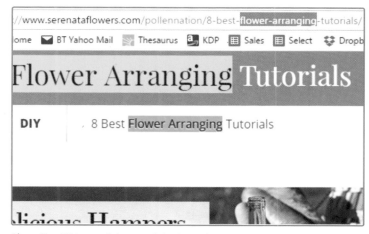

Above: Your URL is a good place to include a keyword.

Titles, Headers, URLs and Tags

Titles, headers, URLs (web page addresses) and meta tags (more on this in the next section) are all good places to include keywords but, as with using them in your content, make sure you place them naturally, and do not overuse them.

LOCATION-BASED KEYWORDS

Search engines are now very location-specialized. They can identify where a user is searching from, and often bring up geo-localized results. For example, if somebody types 'florist' into Google, results near to that person's location rank the highest. If you have a location-specific business, and want to attract local customers, a simple way of ensuring search engines know where you are based is to use place names in your content. For example, instead of writing 'plumbing service', write 'London (or whatever your location is) plumbing service' (more on location-based SEO in 'Building a Trusted Site', page 62).

Above: Search engines now automatically bring up businesses closest to a user's location.

BUILD SEO-FRIENDLY SITES

While search engines use keywords and other criteria to match a search request with relevant content, how a site looks and is structured can also affect its search engine rankings.

MAKING INDEXING EASY

Having good-quality, informative and relevant content is not enough to ensure you rank highly in SERPS. Search engines have to index your content, and for them to do that you need to ensure they are structured in such a way that search engine spiders can crawl them easily.

```html
<!DOCTYPE html>
<!--[if IE 8]>     <html class="ie8" lang="en"> <![endif]-->
<!--[if IE 9]>     <html class="ie9" lang="en"> <![endif]-->
<!--[if gt IE 8]><!-->
<html lang="en-US" prefix="og: http://ogp.me/ns#" class=" td-md-is-chrome">
   <!--<![endif]-->
 ▶ <head>…</head>
 ▼ <body class="home td-blog-cars wpb-js-composer js-comp-ver-4.12 vc_responsive td-boxed-layout" item=
WebPage"> == $0
    ▶ <div class="backstretch">…</div>
    ▶ <div class="td-scroll-up">…</div>
    ▶ <div class="td-menu-background">…</div>
    ▶ <div id="td-mobile-nav" style="min-height: 639px;">…</div>
    ▶ <div class="td-search-background">…</div>
    ▶ <div class="td-search-wrap-mob">…</div>
    ▶ <div id="td-outer-wrap">…</div>
      <!--close td-outer-wrap-->
    ▶ <style type="text/css">…</style>
    ▶ <script type="text/javascript">…</script>
      <!--

              Theme: Newspaper by tagDiv 2016
              Version: 7.2 (rara)
              Deploy mode: deploy

              uid: 5825bef870611

      -->
      <script type="text/javascript" src="http://www.carblog.co.uk/wp-content/plugins/contact-form-7/in
```

Above: Search engines crawl a web page's HTML, not the actual web page as it appears to a human visitor.

SEO Site Structure

Websites and blogs should be constructed in a logical way to make search engine crawling and human navigation easy. They should include certain elements:

- **Home Page:** Usually the main website page. Home pages should link to all the relevant sections of a website or blog.

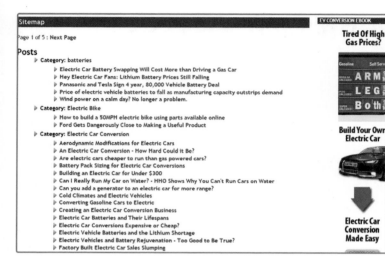

Above: A sitemap contains a list of all the posts and web pages contained on a website or blog.

- **Sitemap:** Lists all the web pages on your website, which users and search engines can use to navigate your website.

- **Headers:** Using the HTML <h1>, <h2> and <h3> tags, all content should include headings and subheadings.

Above: Use <h> tags to create headlines, subheadings and section headings.

Jargon Buster

HTML (the code websites are written in) uses <h> tags to denote headings, <h1> being the largest, and normally the title of a page or post, and <h2> and <h3> tags for subheadings and so on.

Indexable Content

Content needs to be readable to both humans and search engines. While people may be able to read text embedded in images or Flash (animations), search engines cannot. Of course, using images and animations is a great way to engage visitors, but search engines can only use the filename of the media, the link text pointing to it, and the text adjacent to the image to decide upon its content and relevance.

Above: A search engine cannot read text embedded in an image.

Hyperlinked Pages

Search engines require hyperlinks to navigate websites, so make sure every page is linked to either the home page or another web page linked to the home page. Search engines cannot index orphan pages (those that are not linked to).

Hot Tip

You can see the HTML code of any website by pressing Ctrl+U from a PC browser, or going into the Tools/Settings menu on your Mac browser, and looking under 'Developer' for 'Page Source'.

METADATA

Metadata is information used in HTML code that describes aspects of a web page. Some metadata is visible to humans, such as the URL (website address), while other metadata is only used by search engines to help them index pages. When you construct a website or blog, it is crucial to include accurate metadata in the source code. You can use the developer tools of your website or blog content management software (CMS) to add and edit metadata, or enter it straight into the source code (HTML).

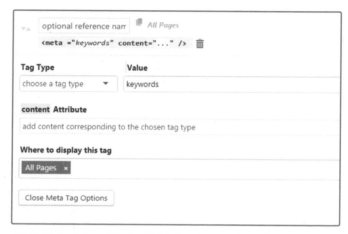

Above: Most website and blogging CMS platforms have simple metadata managers where you can enter meta tags.

META TAGS

When it comes to SEO, the most important metadata comes in the form of meta tags. Meta tags are usually

Above: While title and description tags are visible to users in search results, keyword tags are not.

included near the top of a page in HTML code, and contain all sorts of information for search engines to utilize. There are three main meta tags:

- **Title Tag**: Contains the title or brief summary of a web page.

- **Description Tag**: Describes what a web page is about, including key information and what the content contains.

- **Keyword Tag**: Tells a search engine what the most applicable keywords for that web page are.

The most influential UK automotive blogs
influential-**blogs**.co.uk/list.php?category=**auto** ▾
All of the best British automotive **blogs**, with their social r
details. ... The UK's most influential car/automotive **blogs**

Carscoops : news in the world of automob
www.**cars**coops.com/ ▾
A daily web **blog** with scoops and news from the **auto** ind

Jalopnik - Drive Free or Die

Above: Title tags are the bold blue text in search engine results.

Title Tag

The title tag is the bold blue text that appears on a search engine results page. The title tag can be the name of a website or a brief summary of the content. Title tags should be 50–60 characters long, and it is a good idea to ensure they include keywords, but make sure they read naturally and are not keyword stuffed. Make sure each web page has a different title tag, because duplicates can affect search engine rankings. A title tag should also be snappy and appealing to visitors.

HTML title tag example:
<title>Laptop Repair in London – Low Rates.</title>

Automotive Blogs UK Top 10 | Vuelio

www.vuelio.com/uk/social-media-index/top-10-uk-**auto**motive-**blogs**/ ▼

24 Aug 2016 - The Top 10 Automotive Blog ranking was last updated 24/08/2016. ... From features to finance, The Car Expert is the place to turn for automotive advice and recommendations for any budget. ... Independent motoring site Motor Verso caters to the most devote of **car-enthusiasts by** delivering a ...

Car and Driver Blog: Car News and Photos

blog.caranddriver.com/ ▼

14 hours ago - Read the latest car news and check out newest photos, articles, and more from the Car and Driver Blog.

Above: Description tags should tell people what they will find on the web page.

Description Tag

The description tag is the text that appears on a search engine results page under the title tag. The primary focus of a good description tag is to describe your web page to potential visitors. Description tags should be about 130–160 characters long, and while some search engines do not rank using description tags, it is still a good idea to include a keyword or two, because they are often highlighted if they match a search query, making the description more appealing to a user.

HTML description tag example: <meta name="description" content="We repair laptops throughout the London area. Low prices and free quotes. Contact us now 0800 888 8888."

Keywords Tag

As the name suggests, the keywords tag is where you can tell a search engine what keywords are applicable to the web page. A comma separates keywords and keyword phrases, and while there is no limit to the number of keywords you can include, it is best to stick to between five and 10, depending on the length of content on your page.

HTML keyword tag example: <meta name="keywords" content="laptop repair, computer repair, London laptop repair, computer fix, cheap laptop fix.">

If you have a phone number for your business website, include it in the title or description tag, because some customers prefer to call without needing to click on to a website.

Crewe Florist - Same Day Flower Delivery Order by 1pm
www.hocknellsflorist.co.uk/flower_delivery/Crewe.aspx ▾
Local flowers delivered by hand, by us, no postal flowers, no relay fees, order online
speak to a real florist, by ordering flowers from us you cut out ...

Contact Quiggs Florist | Florist Londonderry Contact Details | Fl
www.quiggsflorist.co.uk/contact-us/ ▾
Fresh flowers hand delivered by a local florist! If you require a very urgent delivery
call 028 7136 6452 and we shall be more than happy to ...

Melksham Florist, Free Local Flower Delivery, Wiltshire Flowers
https://www.wiltshireflowers.org.uk/ ▾
Wiltshire Flowers Melksham, is a top quality florist specialising in hand tied gift bouqu
flowers. Order flowers online or give us a call on Tel ...

Florist London flower shop in London open 24 hours a day
www.flowerstation.co.uk/florist-local-london-shop-delivery/ ▾
Same day florist delivery in London, London florist hand delivered   Monday to Su

Above: If you have a business website, include your phone number in the meta title or description.

Manually Entering Meta Tags

You can enter meta tags straight into the HTML source code if you do not have a metadata manager.

1.   Open up your source code in your CMS.

2.   At the top of the source code (above the <h1> tag), type in '<head>' (without the quotes).

3.   Enter the title, description and keyword meta tags.

4.   Type '</head>' (without the quotes) to close the meta coding, and save the changes to your HTML file.

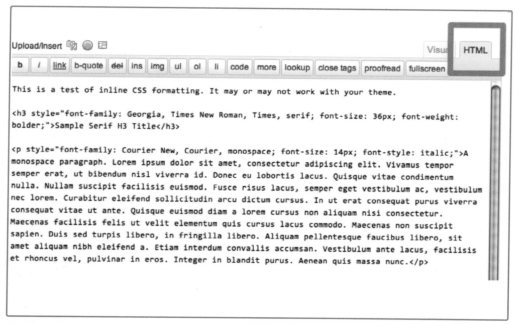

Above: Blogging software, such as WordPress, has a simple-to-use HTML mode.

```
<!DOCTYPE HTML PUBLIC "-//W3C//DTD HTML 4.0 Transitional//EN">
<html>
<head>
<title>All our wooden furniture is water proof.</title>
<meta name="keywords" content="wood, furniture, garden, garden-table, etc">
<meta name="description" content="Official dealer of wooden garden furniture.">

</head>

<body>

Visit our showroom on weekdays from 9 to 5...

</body>
</html>
```

Above: Meta tags entered into source code.

Rich Snippets

Not to be confused with featured snippets, search engines now have a feature you can include in your HTML called rich snippets, which provide additional pieces of information about a web page. We will explore rich snippets in more detail in 'Advanced SEO', page 116.

Minestrone Soup with Pasta, Beans and Vegetables Recipe : R
www.foodnetwork.com › Recipes › Italian

 ★★★★☆ Rating: 4 - 127 reviews - 4 hrs 15 mins
Mar 5, 2013 – Get this all-star, easy-to-follow Food Network **Mine**
Soup with Pasta, Beans and Vegetables recipe from Robin Miller

Minestrone Soup Recipe : Ellie Krieger : Recipes : Food Networ
www.foodnetwork.com › Recipes › Comfort food

 ★★★★★ Rating: 5 - 85 reviews - 45 mins
Mar 16, 2013 – Get this all-star, easy-to-follow Food Network **Min**
Soup recipe from Ellie Krieger.

Minestrone - Wikipedia, the free encyclopedia
en.wikipedia.org/wiki/**Minestrone**
Minestrone is a thick **soup** of Italian origin made with vegetables, often with th

Above: Rich snippets include additional information, such as customer reviews.

BUILDING A TRUSTED SITE

LINKS

Links are what connect the World Wide Web together, so it's no surprise that they are crucial for search engine optimization. Links not only bring in traffic from other websites, but search engines also use them as an indication of trustworthiness and popularity.

VALUE OF LINKS

Ever since search engines first emerged, links have played a crucial role in determining the rank of a website in search engine results. Inbound links are an indication of popularity; the more web pages link to a site, the more popular it is likely to be. Depending on their source, inbound links can also be an indication of trustworthiness and authority, as well as helping search engines to determine what is spam.

Above: Links are what connect the World Wide Web together.

Jargon Buster

Inbound links are another name for backlinks, and are links that come from an external website into your website. Outbound links go the other way.

Quality and Quantity

While the determining factors used by search engine algorithms for ranking a web page or blog are highly complicated, when it comes to links, search engines look at several key aspects:

- **Quantity:** The more links coming into a website, the more popular it is likely to be.

- **Quality:** Links from trusted sources carry more weight than links from less trusted sources.

- **Relevance:** The relevance of a website linking to your web page is also a factor.

Above: Links from authoritative websites such as the BBC carry a lot of weight.

TRUSTWORTHINESS

Search engines work on the idea that the most trusted websites must be those that are the most popular. However, it is not simply a numbers game. Where the links come from is crucial, and can have a large impact on determining your website's trustworthiness and relevance.

Trusted Sources

Links from trusted sources carry the most weight. Respected websites such as Wikipedia, national news organizations or high-ranking websites or blogs are the most valuable. Links from social media and low-ranking websites or blogs carry much less weight.

Relevance

How relevant the website linking to your content is also plays an important role. For instance, if you have a blog that discusses dog grooming, a link from a website that specializes in content about dogs is more valuable than a link from a website or blog that has nothing to do with dogs.

Insert/edit link	✕

Enter the destination URL

URL

Link Text Lorem

☐ Open link in a new window/tab

Or link to existing content ▾

Cancel   Add Link

Above: The more people who link to your website, the more link juice it has.

Jargon Buster

The power of a link coming into your website is known as 'link juice'. The more authoritative and trusted the website linking to yours, the more link juice it provides.

ANCHOR TEXT

In many ways, anchor text is similar to keywords. In essence, anchor text is the clickable text on a web page that activates the link. If a page is using keywords relevant to your content as anchor text, it has far more benefits for SEO than a website that has a simple 'click here' link to your content.

Floristry is the production, commerce and trade in flowers. It arranging, merchandising, and display and flower delivery: W professionals in the trade. Retail florists offer fresh flowers an

Floristry can involve the cultivation of flowers as well as their raw material supplied for the floristry trade comes from the c main flower-only outlets, but supermarkets, garden supply st

Floral design or floral arts is the art of creating flower arrange bouquets and compositions from cut flowers, foliages, herbs, "floral design" and "floristry" are considered synonymous. Flo the retail level. Floristry differs from floristics, the study of dist

Above: Anchor text is the words used to activate the link.

LINK-BUILDING

If you want to improve your search engine rankings, you need to ensure you are getting good-quality inbound links. Unquestionably, link-building is the most challenging aspect of SEO. Where do you get links from? How do you ask for them? You need a link-building strategy, but before you come up with one, you need to understand the different ways of getting links:

- **Natural Links:** Links that people on other websites or blogs give you after reading your content, without you having communicated with them.

- **Outreach Links:** Links that you have acquired through networking, asking people if they could link to your content.

- **Self-Created Links:** Links you have placed on other websites yourself, such as on a comments page or on a social media account.

The Flame Tree Team
@flametreetweet

Flame Tree Publishing: books, calendars, ebooks. See our great blog on art, movies, music, recipes, gothic fiction and more.
blog.flametreepublishing.com

◉ London, UK
🔗 flametreepublishing.com
📅 Joined April 2010

Above: Even links on social media profile pages add link juice.

Building Natural Links

There is only one way to build natural links: to create the best, most engaging content that you can.

- **Linkable Content:** Make sure you are producing content that, once people see it, they will want to share – news and information or multimedia content, for example, is often linked to.

- **Promotion:** You can improve your chances of other people seeing your content if you promote it on social media and community forums.

- **Blogging:** Blogging enables you to produce regular, fresh content, and gives you more opportunities to earn links.

Jargon Buster

Content that attracts a large number of links is known as 'linkbait'. A good example of this is viral videos that can be shared tens of thousands of times.

Above: Blogging enables you to link to your own website and bring in new visitors.

Self-Created Links

You can create your own links on all sorts of websites, such as the comments pages on somebody's blog, or in your social media profile. You need to be wary, because creating lots of self-created links could make search engines believe you are pursuing an aggressive link-building strategy. However, if you regularly comment on a specific blog or forum, especially if it is related to the content on your website, including some self-created links shouldn't hurt, and can have an aggregated effect on SEO.

Above: Include a link to a website address on any forums you sign up to.

Above: Some business websites link to customers in exchange for a reciprocal link on the customer's website.

Building Outreach Links

Convincing other people to link to your website is perhaps the most daunting and challenging aspect of link-building and SEO in general. However, if you really want to boost your search engine rankings, you need to increase the number of links to your website. The best way to do that is to approach other websites and blogs, and ask them for a link. However, you need to identify which websites to ask and what to say.

LINK-BUILDING STRATEGY

Coming up with a link-building strategy can help you identify where to get links from and convince others to link to you. Your link-building strategy should include three factors:

- ○ **Goals:** You do not want to spend your time just endlessly pursuing links, so you need to identify an ultimate goal, which could be to generate enough links to get you higher in the rankings, and to generate a certain number of these naturally.

Hot Tip

If you are running a business website, consider asking your customers or suppliers for a link. You can provide them with a link in return.

- **Identifying Sources**: You need to find people from relevant sources who can provide you with authoritative, trusted links.

- **Convincing People to Link**: Once you have identified people you want links from, you need to find ways to convince them to link to you.

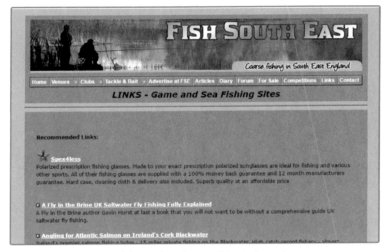

Above: Many bloggers have a links page for websites and blogs in their topic area.

Identifying Link Sources

To identify the best people to approach for links, you need to find the most influential and relevant sources, and find out who links to them.

1. Use a search engine to find websites in your content area – the higher-ranking, the better.

2. Use a backlink checking tool to find all the websites that link to it (see 'Link-Building Tools', right).

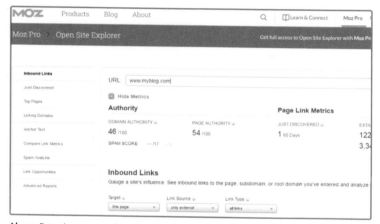

Above: Enter the most popular websites in your topic area into Moz.

2. Visit these websites and blogs, and check to see whether they have relevant or similar content. If so, look for contact details, such as an email address.

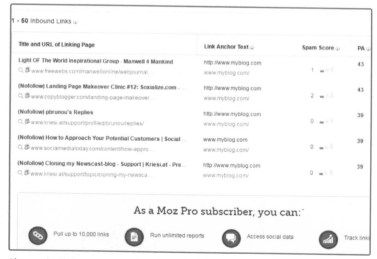

Above: A backlink checker lists all the websites that link to your search.

Convincing People to Link to You

Now comes the hardest part: convincing people to link to your website. The best way to do this is to ensure you are producing content that interests them. Visit their websites and social media channels, and find topics that they care about, and if you have content that you think they may like, send them a link to it. If it engages them, they may blog about it or add you to their links page.

LINK-BUILDING TOOLS

Here are some useful tools for building backlinks:

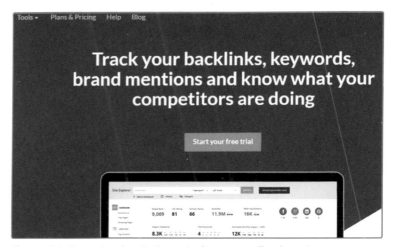

Above: Link-building tools such as Ahrefs are either free to use or offer a free trial.

- **Ahrefs (https://ahrefs.com):** This tool lets you track backlinks, keywords and brand mentions (available with a free trial).

- **Majestic (www.majestic.com):** With this, you can track link information for websites and domains.

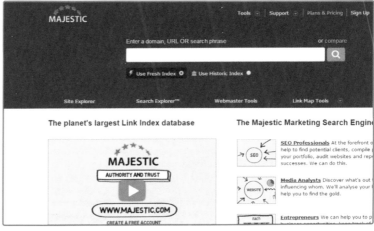

Above: Majestic lets you track link information for websites and domains for a monthly subscription fee.

○ **Moz Linkscape (https://moz.com/researchtools/ose/):** Use this tool to help you research backlinks, discover link-building opportunities and also to find damaging links from spam sites.

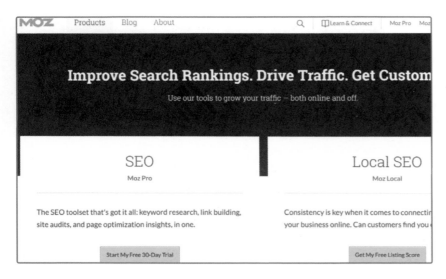

Left: Moz (formerly MozSEO) is one of the most popular SEO and link-building tools available.

OTHER TOP TRUST-BUILDING TIPS

Trust is not just about links. Search engines want to ensure your website or blog provides useful information, and there are steps you can take to encourage search engines to see your website as a trusted resource.

APPEARING TRUSTWORTHY

The internet is not much different from the outside world. Face-to-face communication is important for building a trusting relationship in the non-virtual world. On the web, while you cannot meet face to face, you can create a similar level of trust by creating an open and transparent relationship with your online visitors.

Above: Face-to-face communication builds trust in the outside world.

Faceless Websites

Nothing diminishes trust quicker than an anonymous website, and there are ways you can ensure you are putting a face to your content, and get visitors and consequently search engines to trust you.

- **Websites**: Trusted websites explain who they are. An 'About' page can help visitors know more about you.

- **Blogging**: When writing a blog, always attach your name to your posts. Ideally, think about introducing a photograph of your face, either to your posts or on an 'About' page.

- **Contact Page**: Provide a way for visitors to get in touch with you. Include your business address and phone number, or an email address or contact form, at the very least.

Above: An 'About Us' page can help establish trust with your visitors.

Transparency

People may want to know that your website is genuine. It's not unheard of for people to create fake websites, so make sure that when you register your website domain, you are on a public 'Whois' directory, so people can look you up, if they so wish, using a domain name search engine such as https://whois.net or https://whois-search.com.

OUTBOUND LINK STRATEGY

While inbound links are crucial for gaining trust in search engines, ensuring you are linking out to other reputable, authoritative, trusted and relevant sources also helps establish your website or blog as a trusted resource.

Above: Your outbound links need to be trusted and relevant.

Spam and Dead Links

Never link out to anything that might be considered spam. Always check the authority of the websites to which you link. Furthermore, do regular checks on your outbound links, because dead links can have a detrimental effect on your search engine rankings.

If you have had your products or services reviewed online, link to the reviews. Even an image of scanned copies of offline reviews, such as newspaper articles, can show you are trusted and credible.

404 error

Page not found 🔍

We are sorry but the page you are looking for does not exist.
You could retourn to the homepage or search using the search box below

Above: Links that no longer work can have a detrimental effect on your SEO.

HOUSEKEEPING

Along with checking for dead links, you should do regular housekeeping of your website and its content. Make sure you update any information that may be outdated or no longer relevant. Also, make sure you regularly check for errors, whether factual or typographical, and correct errors as soon as you spot them.

Jargon Buster

A dead link is one that links to a web page that is no longer there. Content being deleted or moved, or a temporary issue with the host's server may cause a dead link.

SECURITY AND PRIVACY

If you request any information from your visitors on your website, such as contact information, you need to make sure users know exactly what you are going to do with that information. Make sure you include 'Privacy' and 'Terms of Service' pages. If you have security measures in place for protecting information, such as SSL (Secure Sockets Layer), make sure you include the certificate.

Above: A privacy and security page should outline what you will do with your visitor's data.

BOUNCE RATE

Bounce rate is the term given to the number of people who visit your website but very quickly leave again. Bounce rate is a good indication that your website is not satisfying a user's search request, and search engines may downgrade websites with high bounce rates.

Even if you manage to get your website high up in the search engine rankings with your SEO endeavours, it will do you little good if visitors are quickly leaving again. Of course, it may well be that your website is very efficient at providing users with the information they are looking for, so you need to determine the reason for your high bounce rate and whether you are satisfying users' needs quickly or frustrating them.

Reasons for High Bounce Rate

High bounce rates can be caused by a number of factors:

- **Site Speed:** People won't wait for a slow web page to load, they'll just move on. You need to ensure your website is fast-loading.

Above: If your website is slow to load, people will soon click away.

- **Poor Layout**: If people cannot find the information they want quickly, they will soon try elsewhere. Ensure your website is well structured, easy to navigate, and the content is clearly laid out.

Above: Pop-ups, particularly pop-up advertisements, really annoy people.

- **Content**: If your content does not provide the information a user is looking for, they will soon move on. Make sure your meta title and meta description provide accurate indicators of your site's content.

Hot Tip

You can use online tools such as Moz or Google Analytics to check your website's bounce rate.

- **Pop-ups**: Avoid pop-up advertisements or anything that a user has to close before they can get to your content.

- **Accessibility**: Your website needs to be just as accessible on mobile platforms as on a computer (see 'Mobile SEO' in 'Advanced SEO', page 118, for tips on making your website mobile-friendly), as you risk being penalized by search engines if it is not mobile-friendly.

LOCAL SEO

Search engines are now local-targeted. When users are searching for businesses or services, search engines like to provide users with the details of those that are in the user's area. So, if you have a business or offer a service, appearing in these local search results can be crucial.

LOCAL LISTINGS

While we have discussed the importance of using localized keywords earlier in this book (see 'Keywords', page 42), for somebody with a business website who wants to attract local customers, by far the most effective thing you can do as regards SEO is to make sure you appear in the local listings. This means that when somebody types in a search related to your business type in your area, you should appear at the top of the results page.

Above: Google's local listings often appear at the top of search results, and include details and a map of nearby businesses.

Google My Business

Google My Business (formerly Google Places) not only ensures local businesses appear at the top of search results, but also makes certain that details such as address and phone number are made available on SERPS, and that the business location is on Google Maps, making it easier for customers to find you.

Signing Up to My Business

If you want your website to appear on Google's local listings, you need to sign up to My Business.

1. If you already have a Google account, sign in to it. If not, create one (click the 'Sign In' box at www.google.co.uk, then click 'Create Account').

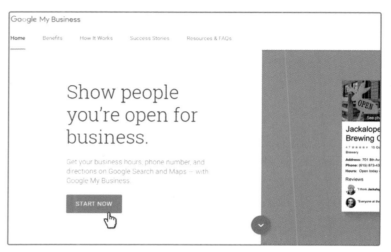

Above: Clicking 'Start Now'.

2. Visit www.google.com/business, and click 'Start Now'.

3. Fill in the details of your business. Be as detailed as possible. (You may find your business appears on a list. If it does, click on it and check/amend the details.)

4. Once filled in, click 'Continue', then 'I am authorized to manage this business', then click 'Continue' again.

Above: Entering your business details. Your business may appear on the list, with its location on the map.

5. Click on 'Mail me my code'. Google will send a verification code in the post to your business location.

6. Enter your verification code, and your website should soon appear in local listings and Google Maps.

Above: Google will want to verify you are the business you are claiming to be.

Hot Tip

Bing has a similar localized business facility to Google's My Business, called Bing Places. You can sign up to this at www.bingplaces.com.

OTHER LOCAL SEO TIPS

There are other ways to help you appear at the top of local search results:

- **NAP**: Make sure your business Name, Address and Phone number are identical in your listings (including format) and on your website. Discrepancies can result in search engines not listing you in their local listings.

- **Reviews**: Appeal to your customers to review your business on websites such as Yelp and Google. User reviews are a measure of trust, and sometimes appear in search results.

- **Focus on Local Links**: Swap links with other local businesses. Local inbound links can improve rankings for localized searches.

- **Social Media**: Use social media to engage and connect with people and businesses in your area.

- **Directories**: Make sure you are listed in any business directories based in your area.

Right: Reviews on websites such as Yelp sometimes appear in search results.

COMMANDING AUTHORITY

BUILD A COMMUNITY

Search engines love to provide authoritative content for their users. The more that people mention your website and brand, and the more that you are discussed online, the more both direct and indirect benefits to SEO, but in order to command authority, you have to first build a community.

SOCIAL MEDIA

The rise of social media has changed the way people use the internet. A social media presence can not only drive traffic to your website, but search engines can also identify how authoritative you are by the number of mentions and conversations that involve your website or brand on social media. Furthermore, people now use social media to find content, rather than just relying on traditional search engines. This makes social media platforms important search engines in their own right

Above: People now use social networks, such as Facebook, to search for content.

Hot Tip

Some search engines favour recent social media posts and place them in the top ranks of search engine results, so the more you post, the more chance you have of appearing at the top of the SERPS.

BUILD A FOLLOWING

Whether it is Twitter, Facebook, LinkedIn or the myriad other social media platforms out there, the number of followers, fans or connections you have can affect your search engine rankings. This means you need to grow your social media base. Do not be tempted to buy followers or likes, because search engines can easily spot fake accounts and distinguish between a regular and a bought following.

TWEETS	FOLLOWING	FOLLOWERS	LIKES
46.5K	1,098	300K	19.4K

Tweets   Tweets & replies   Media

 Lidl UK @LidlUK · Nov 18
The most expensive Christmas Pudding in the world £23,500.

Above: The number of followers and likes on Twitter can demonstrate your authority.

Engaging People

To attract a social media following, you need to do more than just write tweets and Facebook posts. You need to engage people.

○ **Conversations:** Create conversations. Ask questions in your posts, tweets and social media interactions. Join debates and share opinions.

○ **Expertise:** If you have experience or expertise in your topic, share it. Become an authority.

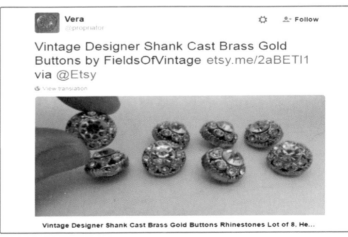

Vera @propriator   ☼ ⚬ Follow

Vintage Designer Shank Cast Brass Gold Buttons by FieldsOfVintage etsy.me/2aBETl1 via @Etsy

View translation

Vintage Designer Shank Cast Brass Gold Buttons Rhinestones Lot of 8, He...

Above: Social media is all about sharing and networking.

- **Reputation**: Be consistent and represent your brand positively. Debate and express opinions by all means, but avoid getting into arguments on social media.

- **Share**: Social media is all about sharing. Share blog posts and news, not just from your own website or business, but from elsewhere too.

BUILDING AUTHORITY

Every time one of your tweets, Facebook posts or other social media interactions is shared, favourited, liked, retweeted or replied to, it raises your authority to search engines. The more it appeals to your audience, the more likely your content is to be shared.

Encouraging Shares

Besides posting the most appealing content you can on social media, there are other ways to encourage shares and interactions with your posts:

- **Share Buttons**: Include share buttons on your website or blog. This makes it easy for people to share your content on social media.

- **Rewards**: Offer rewards, such as entrance to competitions, for social media shares.

- **Surveys**: Use social media surveys or polls to encourage interaction.

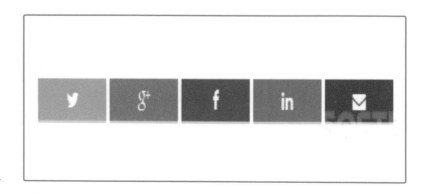

Right: Share buttons on your blog or website encourage people to share.

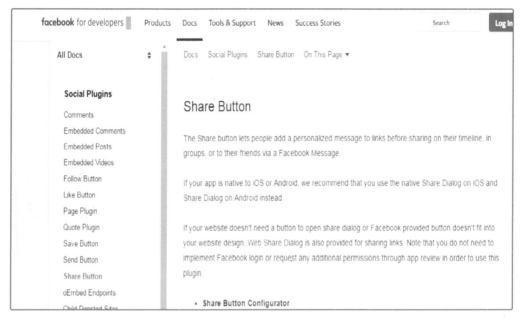

Above: Social networks, such as Facebook, often have instructions and tools for including share buttons on your website.

WHICH SOCIAL NETWORK?

With so many different social networks to choose from, it can be difficult to know which ones to sign up to, but here are some of the most influential:

○ **Facebook**: With over one billion users worldwide, Facebook is the world's most popular social network. You can set up a business page or share blog posts.

○ **Twitter**: The microblogging platform is perfect for sharing links to articles, websites and blog posts, and promoting businesses.

> # Hot Tip
>
> If you write a blog, always share your new posts on social media. Make sure you respond to comments, because this helps keep the conversation going.

○ **Instagram:**
The photo- and
video-sharing
platform has over
300 million users,
and is perfect
for sharing
multimedia
content.

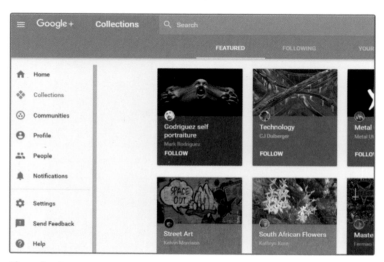

Above: Google+.

○ **Google+:**
Create
communities
with its Circles
feature, and
chat, network
and keep abreast
of what others
in your Google+
network
are doing.

○ **LinkedIn:**
The professional
social media
network makes
connecting
with other
people in your
field easy.

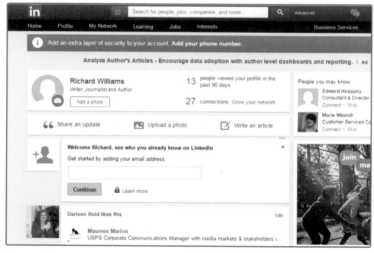

Above: LinkedIn.

Niche Social Networks

With so many users on the main social media networks, it can be hard to get noticed among all that noise, but there are a number of niche platforms that appeal to specific industries and topics, which may make it easier to find an audience.

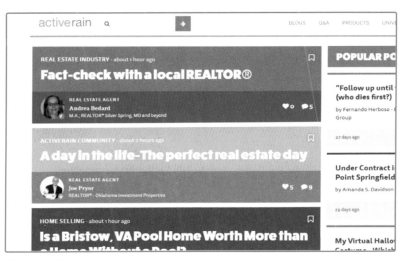

Above: ActiveRain.

- **ActiveRain:** A social network for realtors, estate agents and others in the housing industry.

- **Alignable:** Connects local businesses together.

- **DeviantArt:** A social network for artists and art lovers.

- **Doximity:** A platform dedicated to doctors and physicians.

Above: Doximity.

SOCIAL MEDIA TIPS AND TRICKS

If you want to get the most out of social networks, some of these techniques can help:

Above: Hashtags make it easy for people to search for specific topics.

- ○ **Hashtags**: Learn which hashtags are relevant to your topic or business, because using them helps attract a larger audience.

- ○ **Analyse Content**: What types of social media posts have received the most interactions? What didn't work? Learn what your audience likes.

- ○ **Links**: Use teaser copy to prompt people to click links, such as, 'Guess what's the most popular ... (flowers at weddings, for example).'

- ○ **Images**: A picture is worth a thousand words. Don't just rely on text — images are more appealing and catch people's attention.

Jargon Buster

Some social media networks, such as Twitter, LinkedIn and Instagram, use hashtags. These are words or phrases preceded with a #, which enable you to identify messages on a particular topic.

CREATE POPULAR CONTENT

In order to gain authority, you need people to notice you, and that means learning to satisfy your audience with content they not only want to see but will also share with others.

WHAT IS POPULAR?

While we have discussed the importance of creating quality content (see 'Search-Engine Friendly Content', page 32), ensuring that it is popular is just as important for SEO if you want to encourage shares and interactions. However, it can be more art than science when identifying what content takes off and what doesn't.

Popularity Components

When creating content, you should have several things in mind if you want it to be popular:

○ **Spreadable**: Popular content has to be created in such a way that people will want to share it.

○ **Interest**: You have to appeal to your audience's interests.

Jargon Buster

Content that is shared by a large number of people is known as 'viral content'. However, making something go viral is incredibly difficult.

> **Andrew Malcolm** ✔
> @AHMalcolm
>
> For every retweet this gets, Pedigree will donate one bowl of dog food to dogs in need! ☺ #tweetforbowls
>
> 8:10 PM - 15 Feb 2015
>
> ↩ ↜ 694,021   ♥ 138,199

Above: Some content, such as this donation promotion by Pedigree, goes viral and receives thousands of retweets.

◯ **Brand:** If you are trying to promote your business, product or service, you need to ensure the content is relevant and connected with it in some way.

What Do People Like?

While it can often be hit and miss attempting to create content that is popular or will go viral, there are some types of content that often have a much better chance:

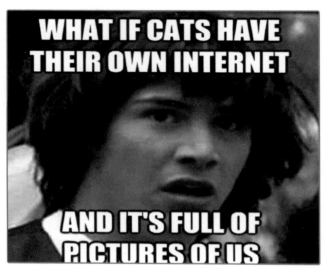

Above: Memes are very popular on social media.

- **Memes**: Images or videos with a humorous nature often spread rapidly around the internet.

- **Videos**: Links to videos are frequently shared. If you can create your own videos, you have far more chance of getting those shares.

- **Infographics**: If you have data or statistics you want to share, infographics (information graphics) are a handy way to communicate them, and are often shared on social media.

Hot Tip

YouTube is the best place to upload videos. The video social networking site makes it easy for people to share videos on other social networks.

Above: Infographics are popular because they are an effective way to relay lots of complicated information in an easy-to-absorb format.

Influencers

Popularity can also depend on who shares your content and with whom you interact. In many professions and topic areas, there are key influencers: those people whom everybody knows and who are considered experts in their field. Identifying these people, sharing content with them, and regularly commenting on their blogs or social media posts will help you become part of their influential sphere.

Above: You can see your Twitter stats at https://analytics.twitter.com.

Analyse

As with all aspects of SEO, when you have created content that has had a lot of shares and interactions, it is worth analysing it to work out what caused it to be popular, then try to repeat that success.

BE NEWSWORTHY

Search engines love news, and so do their users. Putting out newsworthy content can not only give you a lift in search engine rankings, but also help you reach a huge audience if you get coverage in some of the top online news outlets.

WHAT'S NEWS?

When it comes to news content, some people get confused as to what exactly constitutes news, and either make the mistake of issuing content that is not newsworthy, which gets ignored by news sites and resources, or miss opportunities to put out newsworthy content because they do not recognize it as such.

Newsworthy Content

So, what constitutes newsworthy content? In short, anything that is new could be considered news:

- **New Products**: If you have a business and are releasing a new product or service, that is newsworthy content.

Hot Tip

Top news stories related to search topics often appear at the top of the first page of search results.

https://www.carphonewarehouse.com/apple/iphone-6s.html ▾
Looking for the best iPhone 6s deals, contracts and upgrades? We compare the UK's widest range of networks. And if you find it cheaper anywhere else, we'll ...

In the news

Apple to fix 'touch disease' flaw for iPhone 6 Plus
The Guardian · 2 days ago
Apple has acknowledged a significant flaw that causes touchscreens to fail in some iPhone ...

Apple iPhone 6 Plus 'touch disease' flaw: Here's how to get it fixed
Pocket-lint.com · 2 days ago

Apple to fix iPhone 6 Plus 'touch disease' for a fee
BBC News · 2 days ago

More news for iphone

iPhone | John Lewis
www.johnlewis.com/browse/electricals/mobile-phones-accessories/iphone/_/N-7bqw ▾
Apple iPhone 7, iOS 10, 4.7", 4G LTE, SIM Free, 32GB, Gold. ... Apple iPhone 7, iOS 10, 4.7", 4G LTE, SIM Free, 128GB, Silver. ... Apple iPhone 7 Plus, iOS 10, 5.5", 4G LTE, SIM Free, 32GB, Gold

Above: The first page of search engine results frequently shows top news stories featuring search keywords.

○ **Events**: An industry or business event, such as a conference, exhibition or sale, could be considered news.

○ **Promotions**: Use news channels to promote your discounts, giveaways and competitions.

○ **Projects**: News sites love to hear about exciting projects and corporate deals.

○ **Innovations**: New ideas, techniques and technology always make good news stories.

○ **Stories**: Human-interest stories, business achievements and milestones all make worthwhile news content.

Above: Anything that is new can be considered news.

NEWS OUTLETS

Once you have a news story, you need to identify where to send it and which the key news outlets are:

○ **News Organizations**: National news organizations, such as the BBC, Times, Guardian, Telegraph and Huffington Post, all have an online presence, but they usually only pick up the news stories that appeal to a broad audience.

Trade Press: Most industries have their own news organizations that are always looking for news content, and are more likely to publish niche news stories.

Bloggers: News sources do not have to be big-name news outlets. Sending news stories to industry and topic-related bloggers are great ways to reach a specific audience.

Above: Trade magazines, such as The Flower Arranger, are great places to send news on niche subjects.

Above: Google News is a good way of getting your news out there.

Google News

When it comes to SEO, one of the best outlets to get your news noticed is Google News. Google uses a news search algorithm that scours all the news outlets on the web to bring up news for specific keyword searches. Rankings tend to depend on the authority of a news source and how recent the news story is, but getting a mention in a story ranking high on Google News can indirectly bring in large amounts of traffic to a website. However, Google does have quite tight guidelines as to what sorts of news and websites it will include in Google News. There guidelines can be found at: https://support.google.com/news/publisher/answer/40787?hl=en-GB.

PRESS RELEASES

Once you have identified your news content and found some news sources, you may wonder how to send your news to people. Perhaps the simplest and most tried-and-tested method is to send out a press release. This is simply a write-up of your news story, with contact details, images and relevant quotes.

Press Release Websites

Thankfully, the days of having to post or fax your press release to every imaginable news outlet are over. These

Hot Tip

When writing a press release, try to summarize all the key points in the first paragraph, and come up with a catchy headline.

days, all you need to do is send it to a press release website. Many of these distribute it to all the relevant news outlets, as well as publishing it on their own website for people to find.

Press Release Distribution Outlets

How well your news content does can often depend on which distribution outlet you use:

FOR IMMEDIATE RELEASE

Launch of new book store

Local owners open book store for local authors and poets

The Happy Book Store opened on Thursday 15ᵗʰ May 2014 to a wide audience and fully stocked with books from local authors, all with the a launch party including some of the city's most respected and up and coming authors.

The Happy Book store is owned by Steve Davis and Charlie Bromley, they have both run stores in the past and had a great wealth of experience within the publishing world.

Specifically selling books that are independently published by smaller publishing houses and some works which have been self-published by the authors alone, they also sell work from up and coming

Above: There are lots of resources available to help you construct a press release.

○ **PRWeb.com:** Widely considered to be one of the best news distribution websites, PRWeb's prices start at $99, and it offers wide distribution, as well as SEO packages.

Right: PRWeb has a number of different pricing packages.

- **PRLog.org**: A free press distribution service that offers some SEO tools, such as being able to include links and keywords.

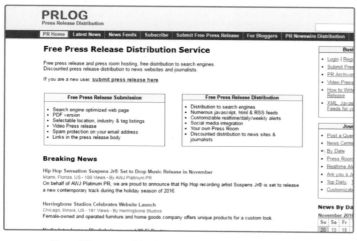

Above: PRLog is one of the best free press release distribution sites.

- **PRNewswire.com**: Prices start at $300, but it has a wide variety of SEO tools and perhaps the widest distribution net.

- **News and PR Agencies**: Organizations such as PA (Press Association), Gorkana and AP (Associated Press) distribute news to other media organizations such as national newspapers, trade magazines and others.

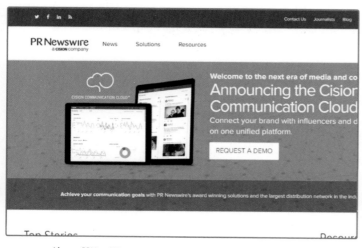

Above: PRNewsWire.

Hot Tip

While many press release distribution services offer you the chance to include links, these may vary in how valuable they are for SEO and may not be worth paying extra for.

KEEP IT FRESH

Search engine rankings fluctuate all the time. As new content emerges, older content can be demoted in SERPS. This means that to remain high in the rankings, you need to keep producing new content to keep things fresh.

FRESHNESS

When it comes to SEO, freshness is simply how new something is. The fresher it is, the better. Search engines want to provide their users with the latest resources and up-to-date information, so freshness matters.

bi-monthly UK magazine with articles on all aspects of floristry, flower arranging and allied crafts, with inspiration for **new** contemporary ideas from around the ...

A Flower Arrangement Inspired by Gerhard Richter - WSJ
www.wsj.com/**articles**/a-**flower-arrangement**-inspired-by-gerhard-richter-1429288812 ▾
17 Apr 2015 - For an April-themed arrangement, floral designer Lindsey Taylor welcomes the rainy season   New York Townhouse Sells for $12 Million Discount   A **Flower Arrangement** Inspired by Gerhard Richter ... Most Popular **Articles** ...

Flower Arranging | Style at Home
www.styleathome.com › Decorating ▾
Flower Arranging. 26 articles. 1 2 ... Last >   Stunning **floral arrangements** that celebrate colour ...
10 fab **floral arrangements** by Carolyne Roehm Jan 7, 2013 ...

The secrets of flower arranging | Life and style | The Guardian
https://www.theguardian.com › Lifestyle › Gardening advice ▾
15 Mar 2015   Floristry at home can be so much more than plonking supermarket ... The secret of a perfect hand-tied arrangement is the spiral, where each **new** stem is ... Very odd to write an **article** about a visual outcome without including ...

Flower Arranging and Floral Art - how to articles from wikiHow
www.wikihow.com › Home › Categories › Hobbies and Crafts › Crafts ▾
wikiHow has **Flower Arranging** and Floral Art how to **articles** with step-by-step   Arrange a Ball of Flowers with an Oasis ... Choose Flowers for a **New** Baby ...

Above: Search engines put a lot of importance on newness. Blog posts and news stories often have the date next to them in search results.

Fresh Content

Continually adding content to your website or blog is one of the most important ways to stay authoritative and relevant. Fresh content helps convince search engines that your content is up to date. Not posting something for a long period may result in a drop in search engine rankings.

Hot Tip

When writing fresh content, don't just rewrite or rehash older articles or web pages. Focus on things that are recent, such as the latest developments in your industry or topic area.

Fresh Websites

It's not just your content that should be regularly updated. You should also revamp your website or blog every few years. Search engines may consider a website that hasn't been updated for a long time to be stale and inactive, and hold less authority. Furthermore, revamping your website is appealing to visitors too. Websites have fashion cycles, like everything else. What may have looked modern and cutting-edge a few years ago may now look staid and out of date.

Above: Website design can quickly go out of date.

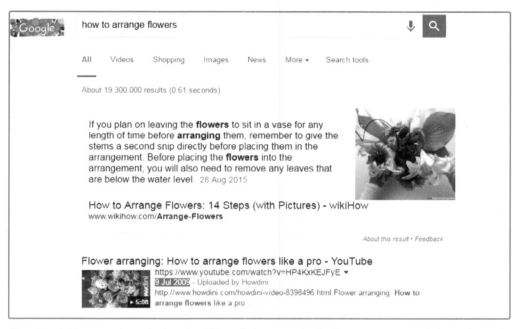

Above: Not all old content is demoted in the rankings. If it is still relevant, trusted and authoritative, even content that's several years old can remain high in the rankings.

FRESH VERSUS EVERGREEN

Just because search engines love freshness, it doesn't mean you have to replace all your old content and web pages. Older web pages that still receive lots of visitors and continue to be relevant, informative, trusted and authoritative may still appear high in the rankings, and could be bringing in traffic for a long time to come. The key is to monitor your web pages, and replace those that no longer have appeal to either visitors or search engines.

Jargon Buster

In SEO, evergreen content is simply that which remains useful and authoritative for a long period, continues to attract visitors and links, and appears high in the rankings.

http:// www.

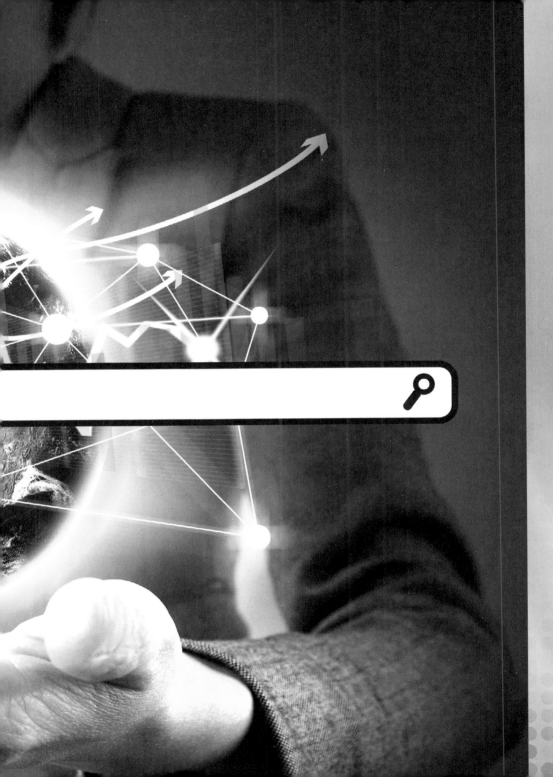

ADVANCED SEO

BEYOND SEARCH ENGINES

Traditional search engines are not the only places people do their searches. All sorts of websites and online platforms have their own search engines for which you may need to optimize content.

VENDOR WEBSITES

These days, many businesses sell products online via third-party vendor platforms, including various internet-based stores:

- **Amazon:** The world's largest retail giant, which sells everything from fruit and vegetables to clothes, electronic items and digital content.

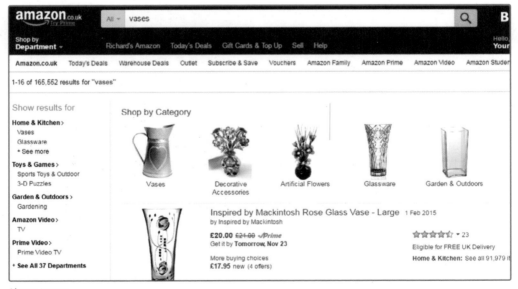

Above: Amazon.

Hot Tip

If you have a product page on Amazon, eBay or other third-party website, don't forget to link to your main website, and also link to your vendor page from your website.

Above: eBay.

- **eBay:** The auction website where vendors can sell both new and used items.

- **App Stores:** Stores such as Google Play (https://play.google.com) and the Apple App Store (https://itunes.apple.com) allow private vendors to sell digital content such as apps, music and e-books.

Above: Apple App Store.

Service Directories

Online retail stores are not the only places small businesses can use to find customers. There are various online directories that enable tradespeople and other professions to advertise their services:

- **www.trustatrader.com**: Enables tradespeople, such as plumbers and builders, to set up a company profile and advertise their services, while consumers can comment and make recommendations.

- **www.ratedpeople.com**: Customers can create a job, for which tradespeople can bid. Also provides a rating system based on customer experience.

- **www.guru.com**: A place where customers can find freelancers such as writers, graphic designers or engineers.

- **www.checkaprofessional.com**: A platform for professionals such as solicitors or accountants.

PRODUCT AND PROFILE PAGES

On many third-party vendor sites, people selling products or services are able to set up a product or profile page, outlining what it is they are selling. As with a website or blog, these pages should be optimized for searches:

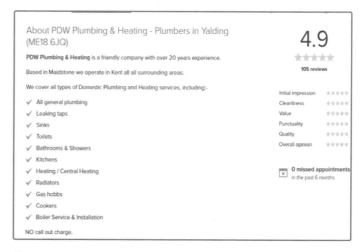

About PDW Plumbing & Heating - Plumbers in Yalding (ME18 6JQ)

4.9
★★★★★
105 reviews

PDW Plumbing & Heating is a friendly company with over 20 years experience.

Based in Maidstone we operate in Kent all all surrounding areas.

We cover all types of Domestic Plumbing and Heating services, including:-

- ✓ All general plumbing
- ✓ Leaking taps
- ✓ Sinks
- ✓ Toilets
- ✓ Bathrooms & Showers
- ✓ Kitchens
- ✓ Heating / Central Heating
- ✓ Radiators
- ✓ Gas hobbs
- ✓ Cookers
- ✓ Boiler Service & Installation

NO call out charge.

Initial impression	★★★★★
Cleantiness	★★★★★
Value	★★★★★
Punctuality	★★★★★
Quality	★★★★★
Overall opinion	★★★★★

0 missed appointments in the past 6 months

Above: Trust a Trader lets users leave reviews on a trader's profile page.

- **Keywords**: Make sure you include keywords on your product or profile page describing your product or services.

- **Location**: If you are a tradesperson, include the areas in which you work to help people's search requests.

- **Categories**: Some vendor sites place products and services into different categories; ensure you use the most relevant categories for your products and services if using these sites.

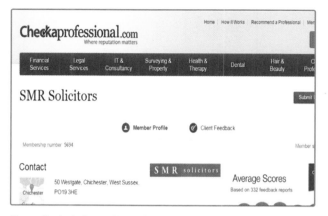

Above: Check a Professional lets professionals set up a profile page based on their profession and location.

Internal and External Search

Product and profile pages on third-party websites are often not only searchable on that particular website, but can also be found using regular search engines. Amazon and eBay pages, for instance, often appear high in Google search results if they are properly optimized, so you need to think about search requests via both the vendor website and general search engines.

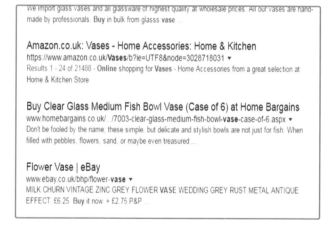

Above: Amazon and eBay pages often appear on Google and other search results pages.

Social Media

As discussed earlier in this book, many people now use the search functions on social media to find information, products and services, so make sure your Facebook, Twitter or Google+ pages are all optimized for search, and linked to your website and product pages.

DEVELOPING YOUR SEO

Now you know the basics of SEO, it's time to look at some of the more advanced methods of optimizing your website to bring in more traffic, and the different ways you can ensure your visitors are there to stay.

LANDING PAGES

Visitors may enter your website on almost any page, depending on what they have searched for. It may be a product page, the home page or your blog. However, to improve your SEO, it can be a good idea to set up specialized web pages that are optimized for specific searches. These are known as landing pages.

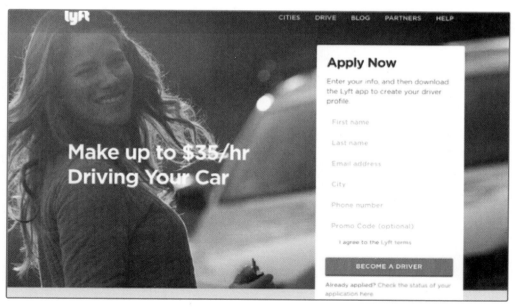

Above: An example of a landing page.

Setting Up a Landing Page

In order for search engines to find your landing page, they should be linked to the site index, but they do not necessarily need to be accessible from your other web pages or home page. This is because they should serve a specific function:

- **Click-through Page**: Landing pages that funnel users to another web page, such as a shopping cart or enquiry page.

- **Lead Generation Page**: Designed to capture user information, such as contact details, that you can follow up later. These typically offer a promotional prize for filling in a form, such as a free trial, contest entry or white paper.

Left: Landing pages are often designed to get users to provide information or buy something.

RICH SNIPPETS

Rich snippets are metadata designed not just to allow search engines to gain a better understanding of the contents of your web page, but also allow searchers to see specific information not normally available in a search, such as reviews, event times and even playable music files, which appear beneath your description on a search engine results page.

Above: Cinemas often use rich snippets to display show times.

Schema.org

Rich snippet information is added to a web page's code in HTML. In order to use rich snippets, an alliance has to be set up to ensure all search engines can benefit from a shared rich snippet vocabulary. A full list of the sorts of information you can include, and the code required to use rich snippets, is available at http://schema.org.

FOLLOW/NO FOLLOW LINKS

We've discussed the importance of linking to authoritative and relevant sources on your website or blog earlier in this book (see 'Building a Trusted Site', page 62). However, there may be occasions when you wish to link to a website that you cannot guarantee is trusted – for example, you may allow people who comment on your blog to link to their website. For this reason, you can use 'no follow' links, which are ignored by search engine bots, so you are not penalized in the search engine rankings.

Using No Follow

A no follow link simply has rel="nofollow" entered into the HTML.

- **Follow Link:** <a href="http://www.examplesite.com"> Example</a>

- **No Follow Link:** <a href="http://www.examplesite.com" rel="nofollow"> Example</a>

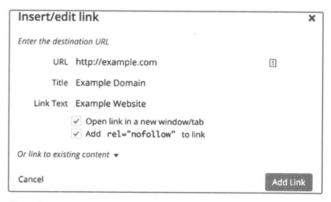

Above: Some content management systems, such as WordPress, enable you to change links from follow to no follow.

MOBILE SEO

More and more people are now accessing the internet on their mobile phones. If your website is not mobile-friendly, you are not only frustrating mobile users who may click away, but search engines are now penalizing websites that do not provide a good mobile experience.

MAKING A MOBILE-FRIENDLY SITE

There are different methods of ensuring your website runs efficiently on mobile devices:

- **Responsive**: Perhaps the easiest method, where your content management system (CMS) reorganizes the content, depending on what type of device is requesting it.

- **Mobile Site**: A completely separate website hosted on a subdomain that is designed around the smaller widths of mobile devices.

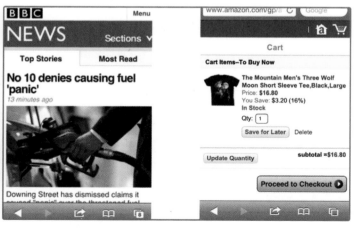

Above: Mobile versions of web pages are narrower.

Jargon Buster

A subdomain is a division of a website's main domain – for example, www.m.example.com would be a mobile subdomain of www.example.com.

Responsive CMS

Various content management systems are available that create mobile versions of your website, depending on the device that is being used:

Above: Websites such as https://themeforest.net provide WordPress mobile themes.

- **Wordpress (http://wordpress.org):** Various WordPress themes are available that enable responsive website design.

- **SquareSpace (www.squarespace.com):** A low-cost ($8/£5 per month), WYSIWYG (What You See Is What You Get) CMS.

Above: Wix can help you create a mobile-responsive website.

- **Wix (www.wix.com):** Another WYSIWYG CMS that enables you to build a free website that should work on both computers and mobile devices.

Designing a Mobile Site

If you decide to design a completely separate website for mobile devices, you need to take several things into account:

- **Size:** Mobile devices are narrower. This means your website needs to be designed accordingly to fit on to a modern mobile device.

Content: Because the width of your mobile site will be much narrower, you may not fit all the same content on, so you need to decide what is crucial to include and what you can omit.

Navigation: Sidebars and links running along the top of a page do not translate well on to a mobile device, so you may need to include a menu system.

Hot Tip

https://testmysite.thinkwithgoogle.com/ lets you test how mobile-friendly your website is and even offers free reports on how to improve mobile speed and accessibility.

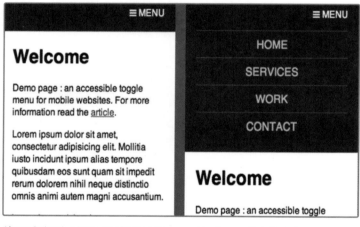

Above: Rather than have a lot of links on the top or side of a page, it's better to have a menu on a mobile website.

Images: Image sizes and ratios may not fit on a mobile device, so you may have to adjust images to ensure they are mobile-friendly.

Speed: A web page has to be quick to load and as some mobile devices are not as powerful as computers, certain elements, such as images and multimedia, may inhibit page-loading speed.

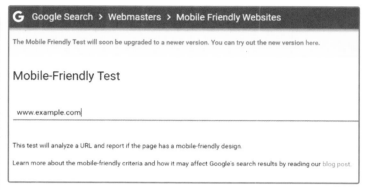

Above: Google's mobile-friendly checker.

Checking Your Mobile Site

If you are unsure whether your web pages are mobile-friendly, one of the easiest ways to find out is to ask Google to check them for you.

1. Visit www.google.co.uk/webmasters/tools/mobile-friendly/.

2. Enter your web page URL (web address).

3. Google analyses your page (this may take a few seconds) and tells you the results.

Making Changes

If your website is not mobile-friendly, you may just need to make some simple changes, such as altering the width of the content, reorganizing the page or shrinking certain elements, such as images.

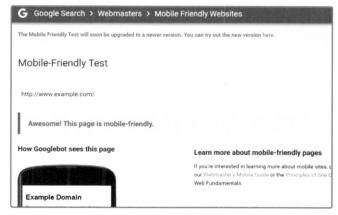

Above: Google tells you whether your web page is mobile-friendly.

Hot Tip

Mobile devices don't just include phones. You need to ensure your website runs on tablets and other handheld devices too.

ANALYTICS, PLUG-INS AND PROBLEMS

Once you have optimized your website, blog or other internet pages for search engines, you need to continually monitor your performance and fix any issues, to ensure your rankings and visitor numbers do not drop.

MONITORING SUCCESS

While many of the basic SEO tips and techniques discussed in this book are evergreen, and should provide a continued boost in page rankings, search engines quite often move the goalposts and change their algorithms, which can cause fluctuations in your rankings. Furthermore, simple little mistakes and minor issues can sometimes cause large drops in rankings once spotted by search engine bots.

Special Offers 20% off · Free Next Day Delivery · Birthday Flowers · International Delivery

Debenhams Online Florist - With Next Day Delivery
Ad www.debenhamsflowers.com/store ▾
Gorgeous Bouquets from £19.99. All with 7 Day Freshness Guarantee
Free Delivery · Add a Message for Free · Sunday Flower Delivery
Types: Roses, Lilies, Tulips, Freesias, Gerberas
Add Chocolates for Free · Flowers By Post · Rainbow Flowers · Designer Flowers · Next Day Delivery

Fresh Flowers Delivered Today - Quality Fresh Flower Delivery
Ad www.iflorist.co.uk/order-by/3pm ▾
4.0 ★★★★☆ rating for iflorist.co.uk
Each bouquet individually crafted by our skilled florists. Order online today
Beautiful Flowers · Free Sunday Delivery · Flowers From £14.90 · Lovingly Created

Searches related to florist

tunbridge wells florist delivery   florist camden road tunbridge wells
colonnade florist tunbridge wells   darling & wild tunbridge wells
mrs florist tunbridge wells   the flower basket florists tunbridge wells
florist tunbridge wells high street   mrs florist voucher code

Gooooooooooogle ›
1 2 3 4 5 6 7 8 9 10   Next

Above: For many people, their SEO goal is to get on page one of Google, but staying there is another challenge.

Troubleshooting

After your SEO efforts, if you haven't found any improvements or you have noticed a drop in rankings, it's a good idea to audit your web pages to ensure they abide by search engine rules and are properly optimized. When you audit your website, you are looking for various things that could cause SEO issues:

○ **Keywords and Metadata:** Check the density of your keywords and whether you are using the correct meta tags.

- **Performance**: How your website is performing in specific keyword searches, its rankings, and its mentions and interactions on social media.

- **Links**: Who is linking in, what their authority is, and whether there are any dead links on your website.

- **Content**: Ensuring your content is unique and not duplicated elsewhere.

Tools and Plug-Ins

Along with some of the SEO tools mentioned earlier in this book (see 'Building a Trusted Site', page 62), there are other tools and plug-ins that are useful for analysing and monitoring your SEO:

- **Google Webmaster Tools (www.google.com/webmasters):** Google provides an array of free SEO tools to check all SEO aspects of your website.

- **www.brokenlinkcheck.com:** Checks for broken and dead links.

Above: Duplicate content, either internally or on an external website, damages your SEO.

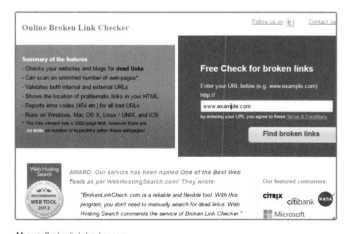

Above: Brokenlinkchecker.com.

Above: Raventools.com.

- **https://raventools.com:** A paid-for tool (from $99/£60 per month) that can perform a complete SEO audit of your website.

- **www.seoreviewtools.com:** A free online service that includes an array of tools to check links, duplicate content and other aspects of SEO.

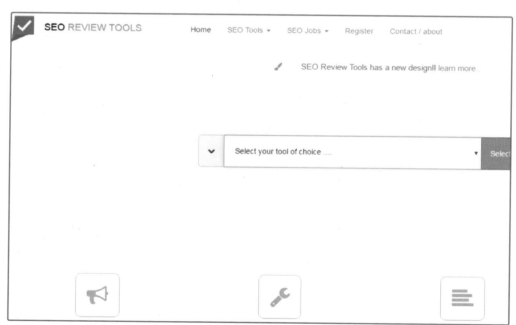

Above: SEOReviewTools.com.

SEO TROUBLESHOOTING CHECKLIST

Even if you have followed all the rules and principles of SEO, sometimes things may not seem as though they are improving. If this happens, there are several features you should check:

- **Keywords**: Ensure you are targeting the right keywords.

- **Duplicate Pages**: Make sure you haven't inadvertently duplicated a web page, especially the home page.

- **404 Errors**: Are any of your internal links broken?

404
NOT FOUND.

Above: Make sure there are no 404 errors on your website.

- **Tags**: Make sure you are using tags correctly and are not duplicating them.

- **Content**: Make sure you are providing relevant, trusted and authoritative content.

Jargon Buster

If your browser cannot find a web page you have linked to, it responds with a page indicating a '404, not found' error.

USEFUL WEBSITES AND FURTHER READING

WEBSITES

www.support.google.com
Contains links to help forums with useful information on web analytics and web design, including an SEO Guidebook that outlines both basic and advanced SEO techniques.

www.searchengineland.com
Collection of up-to-date articles offering several perspectives on the how-tos of SEO technology and current event affairs related to it.

www.moz.com/blog
Collection of blogs where users can publish advice, research and insights as well as ask questions concerning emerging SEO technology.

www.seobook.com
Website dedicated to providing introductory explanations on SEO as well as tools, news and philosophies integrating marketing strategies and web analytics.

www.searchenginejournal.com
Online articles detailing the relationship between social media, e-commerce and SEO and providing advice on blogging and content creation.

www.seochat.com
Online community with forums allowing users – both beginners and professionals – to share knowledge on improving their SEO strategies.

www.mattcutts.com/blog
Blog of a software engineer from Google providing information on SEO in relation to Google and general advice on website design and computer software technology.

www.marketingland.com
Series of articles about online marketing strategies and integrated marketing analytics in the context of optimizing website investments and performance.

FURTHER READING

Beasley, Michael, *Practical Web Analytics for User Experience: How Analytics Can Help You Understand Your Users*, Morgan Kaufmann, 2013

Clifton, Brian, *Advanced Web Metrics with Google Analytics*, Sybex, 2012

Enge, Eric and Spencer, Stephan, *The Art of SEO: Mastering Search Engine Optimization*, O'Reilly Media, 2015

Jantsch, John and Singleton, Phil, *SEO for Growth: The Ultimate Guide for Marketers, Web Designers & Entrepreneurs*, SEO for Growth, 2016

Kaushik, Avinash, *Web Analytics 2.0: The Art of Online Accountability and Science of Customer Centricity*, Sybex, 2009

Kershen, Jerry, *SEO Marketing: 10 Proven Steps to Search Engine Optimization Traffic from Google*, CreateSpace Independent Publishing Platform, 2016

Mangold, Benjamin, *Learning Good AdWords and Google Analytics*, Loves Data, 2015

Odden, Lee, *Optimize: How to Attract and Engage More Customers by Integrating SEO, Social Media, and Content Marketing*, John Wily & Sons, 2012

Lewis, Rhys and Laing, Roger, *Design Your Own Website (Made Easy)*, Flame Tree Publishing, 2010

Stevens, Kevin, *Social Media Mastery: Why Social Media Matters For Your Business & SEO 2016*, CreateSpace Independent Publishing Platform, 2016

INDEX